The Velveteen Principles

The Velveteen Principles

A Guide to Becoming Real

Hidden Wisdom from a Children's Classic

Toni Raiten-D'Antonio

Health Communications, Inc.
Deerfield Beach, Florida

www.hcibooks.com

Please note—The names and identifying characteristics of therapy clients and some others mentioned in this text have been changed to protect their privacy.

Library of Congress Cataloging-in-Publication Data

Raiten-D'Antonio, Toni, 1955–

  The velveteen principles : a guide to becoming real : hidden wisdom from a children's classic / Toni Raiten-D'Antonio.

    p. cm.

  ISBN 0-7573-0211-4

    1. Self-actualization (Psychology) 2. Bianco, Margery Williams, 1880–1944. Velveteen rabbit. I. Title.

  BF637.S4R345 2004

  158.1–dc22

                                                    2004054011

Publisher: Health Communications, Inc.
      3201 S.W. 15th Street
      Deerfield Beach, FL 33442-8190

Cover and inside design by Larissa Hise Henoch
Inside book formatting by Dawn Von Strolley Grove

For Michael (the Boy who made me *Real*),
Elizabeth and Amy

CONTENTS

ACKNOWLEDGMENTS

The feelings and thoughts that inspired this book came to me many years ago. For more than a decade I nurtured and refined the concepts it reveals and worked on the best way to communicate them. Friends and family encouraged me, but it wasn't until I began working with experts in publishing that all my ideas and ideals came to take shape as a book. Although my name is the only one to appear on the cover, these allies contributed much to the work that bears my name:

My agent, David McCormick, helped me, a first-time author, present my concept for a book in a way that was clear and true, and found me the best publisher for my work. At Health Communications I received support from Peter Vegso and Tom Sand, who saw the potential in my idea. Many thanks go to Bret Witter, who shaped my writing and the entire content of this book in a very *Real* way. No one has had a more generous editor. I was also blessed by HCI designers Larissa Hise Henoch and

Dawn Von Strolley Grove who, inspired by William Nicholson's original art, made this such a beautiful book.

I also received support from Antoinette Kania, my former dean at Empire State College, and from colleagues, including the one who teased me by calling the project Velveeta Cheese. And I was both inspired and motivated by my students and psychotherapy clients. My work with them teaches me more than they will ever know.

Finally, I must acknowledge Margery Williams and her creation, *The Velveteen Rabbit*. I am grateful for her wisdom and how she moved me to discover the Velveteen Principles and strive to always be *Real*.

INTRODUCTION

Tattered and taped, with the name "Amy" penciled onto the dustcover in a wobbly three-year-old's hand, my copy of *The Velveteen Rabbit* sits on a shelf in my office near great works in psychology and art. Many of my colleagues— other psychotherapists and professors—would be surprised to hear that this children's book occupies such a place of honor. It does so because it has been vital to my work with hundreds of people. In fact, few sources have meant more to me than this little fable.

First published in 1922, the book follows life in a little boy's nursery where a new arrival, a stuffed bunny covered with inexpensive fabric, copes with the insecurity of being compared with the other playthings. As Margery Williams writes, "He was naturally shy, and being only made of velveteen, some of the more expensive toys quite snubbed him." While he longed to fit in with his peers, the Rabbit hoped even more to become special to the Boy.

Abandoned after the excitement of Christmas, the Rabbit is soothed by the wise, old Skin Horse, who predicts that the Boy will eventually love him. The horse is right, and the Velveteen Rabbit is selected to comfort the Boy through a terrible illness. The Boy's relationship with the bunny and the experiences they share transform it from a toy into something the Skin Horse calls *Real*. To paraphrase the horse, *Real* is what happens when you become your true self—not a contrived, shiny, pretend thing—and are loved despite, and maybe even because of, your imperfections.

A casual reading would lead anyone to conclude that Margery Williams had written a charming, kind and sentimental story. But *The Velveteen Rabbit* is much more than a heartfelt tale. It is a classic parable, with the subtle power to provoke our deepest desires and inspire reflection. It reminds us of basic truths about our heartfelt longings. We all hope to live through life's challenges and grow beautiful and valuable and loved for what we are on the inside, for our *Real* selves.

This book, *The Velveteen Principles,* combines the wisdom of Margery Williams's story with insights from my own experiences as a woman, a psychotherapist, a wife, a teacher and a mother. Although it is just a children's book, *The Velveteen Rabbit* suggests a fairly radical view of the self and of society. It promotes the value of love, empathy and compassion and encourages us to struggle against what is artificial, mechanical and cold. The same is true for this book. It urges you to see the many ways in which you are pressured to abandon what is *Real,* the price you may pay if you do, and the merits of reclaiming everything that makes you a unique and *Real* individual.

The principles I offer are not found in Williams's text, but they are based on the values she made clear through her characters. They are intended to help you to become and stay *Real.* Of course, this book is not a universal prescription for happiness and fulfillment. But in a time when the pace, insecurities and stress of daily life can swamp us, and too many of us "break easily, or have sharp edges," it points to a safe and steady course toward peace, self-acceptance and true love.

To Be Real
in a World of Objects

began to formulate the Velveteen Principles in a most unlikely place. I was at my doctor's office for a routine checkup. I looked up from a glossy, waiting-room magazine, which was full of images of smiling, perfect-looking people, and noticed that it was hard to tell that any of the patients around me were sick, worried or defective in any way. Well-dressed and smiling, we were all trying to look good, just like the people in my magazine.

Then the outside door swung open and a wheelchair-bound woman in her mid-seventies entered, pushed by a man of the same age who was obviously her husband. After stopping at the receptionist's station, they came into the waiting area.

She was bright-eyed but obviously quite ill. Her hands shook, and she breathed with the help of an oxygen tank. She wore no makeup. Red splotches and blue veins were visible through her pale, wrinkled skin. And her clothes were not the least bit feminine or fashionable. She was everything I had been taught to avoid becoming—weak, unhealthy, dependent and unconcerned about the impression she made on others.

Her husband, a white-haired man dressed in khaki pants and a flannel shirt, was small, alert and quite fit.

He had pushed her wheelchair with relative ease and then knelt next to her. He pushed back the sleeve of his shirt, revealing a very old tattoo of a buxom young woman—maybe it was Betty Grable—and stroked his wife's hair. As he adjusted the plastic tubing for her oxygen supply, he spoke softly in his wife's ear. Whatever he said made her smile.

As I peeked over my magazine I became strangely jealous. Here she was, at the end of her life, physically debilitated and struggling. But she was not shy or embarrassed. Instead, she exuded a peaceful sense of certainty about who she was and her inherent value. It was clear that her husband adored her and cherished every moment they spent together. I considered his tattoo and thought of the time when he was young and probably quite obsessed with pretty women. And who knows, maybe his wife was once the girl who had fulfilled his fantasy. But in the moment I witnessed, what he loved was the true and essential person inside the body, the invisible beauty he may not have seen in younger years.

In the weeks after seeing that couple in the doctor's office I struggled to understand why I had been so envious. I had a husband who loved me. I felt good about my work and about my two children, Amy and Elizabeth. But I felt, deep in my heart, there was something that older woman possessed that I wanted. It was there in her face, and in the way she interacted with her husband, but I just couldn't name it.

The answers we need often come to us at unpredictable moments and from surprising sources. This happened to me on a summer evening as I prepared dinner. I was in the kitchen, taking vegetables out of the refrigerator and grabbing pots and pans from the cupboard while my daughters sat together reading on the sofa in the next room. Elizabeth, age six, was reading to two-year-old Amy. Amy had her favorite blanket in her hand, her best bear, Lauren, in her lap and her thumb in her mouth. Elizabeth's stuffed bear, Ted, was propped next to her. They had reached page sixteen of *The Velveteen Rabbit,* Margery Williams's story, which was one of their favorites.

What is REAL asked the Rabbit one day, when they were lying side by side near the nursery fender, before Nana came to tidy the room. "Does it mean having things that buzz inside you and a stick-out handle?"

"Real isn't how you are made," said the Skin Horse. "It's a thing that happens to you. When a child loves you for a long, long time not just to play with, but REALLY loves you, then you become Real."

"Does it hurt?"

"Sometimes," said the Skin Horse, for he was always truthful. "When you are Real you don't mind being hurt."

"Does it happen all at once," he asked, "or bit by bit?"

"It doesn't happen all at once," said the Skin Horse. "You become. It takes a long time. That's why it doesn't happen to people who break easily, or have sharp edges or who have to be carefully kept. Generally, by the time you are Real, most of your hair has been loved off, and your eyes drop out and you get loose in the joints and very shabby. But those things don't matter at all, because once you are real you can't be ugly, except to people who don't understand."

In the kitchen, I was suddenly flooded with emotion and understanding. The Rabbit and the Skin Horse, I realized, were talking about the difference between superficial beauty and the kind of *Real,* inner beauty that we all possess as unique human beings. They were saying that in a life well-lived, where we are true to ourselves, all the struggles and challenges only make us more *Real* and more loveable. Others can see this quality in us, and make us even more *Real* with their love and nurturing.

At last I understood my reaction to the older woman at my doctor's office. She was *loose in the joints.* Her hair was thinning, and her clothes were shabby. But she showed no anxiety, no shame, no worry. She accepted herself fully. She knew she was precious and irreplaceable. She was *Real.* She loved and accepted herself as a

Real, and therefore imperfect, person.

The scene at the doctor's office was made all the more poignant by the fact that the woman's *Real* value was clear to her husband as well. To him she could never be ugly, because she was simply herself. At a moment when anyone else might have been supremely self-conscious, he was so *Real* that he was almost carefree. He had thoroughly overcome the superficial attitude reflected in his old tattoo and come to adore his wife for her deepest, inner self.

As the pages of *The Velveteen Rabbit* turn, the main characters teach us how to find the peace that comes when we focus on what matters most in life: love, relationships, and empathy for ourselves and others. The Skin Horse is a wise and experienced elder who is generous with what he has learned. The Rabbit is, like all of us, insecure and searching for his place in the world, a place he eventually finds in a rather unexpected new life.

As in so many children's books, the human beings in Margery Williams's tale are mostly oblivious to the intense drama affecting the toys in the nursery. In this case, the little Velveteen Rabbit stays with his owner—the Boy—as he suffers through scarlet fever. When the Boy recovers, the doctor insists that the bunny—"a mass of scarlet fever germs!"—be replaced. Though the Rabbit is discarded, it is not the end of the story. As he lies in the yard waiting to be burned with the trash, the Rabbit is transformed from a toy that was *Real* only to the Boy into an actual living creature who is *Real* for all to see. He hops off to live a splendid life with other *Real* rabbits, who become his friends. The words of the Skin Horse, who was wise, secure and content, are proven true. Being *Real* transforms us.

Out in the living room, Elizabeth and Amy paused and looked at their own stuffed animals. Elizabeth's bear, Ted, was missing an eye. The white fur of Amy's bear was dingy gray. Its pink thread nose was a little ragged. The two stuffed animals had both been loved so much, and so deeply, that the girls agreed that they must be *Real*. What was so obvious to my young daughters— that you don't have to be perfect to be worthy—was a revelation to me.

A Realistic Point of View

Over the next few weeks I noticed that the message of *The Velveteen Rabbit* had stirred some long-standing and painful feelings. Even though my life was good, at least as other people might measure it, I didn't possess the confidence, the completeness, the self-awareness of that woman in the wheelchair. As a young woman, mother, wife and professional, I was filled with insecurity and self-doubt. Every day I wore the façade of being sure of myself, but deep inside, I wasn't sure of anything. I wasn't completely *Real*.

Understanding the importance of being *Real* gave me a new perspective, what I would call a more *Realistic* point of view, which slowly changed me. I started by trying to quiet that endlessly self-critical part of myself, the part that dwells on supposed flaws. After all, no one is perfect in a mechanical sort of way, and it's self-destructive to pick on yourself for being human. I also began to embrace the quirky pieces of myself—my interest in art and my sense of humor, for example—and realized that I could be loved just as I am.

Once you recognize the value of being *Real,* you can begin to see that you don't have to live the way everyone else lives. When this truth dawned on me, I started to create a customized life that nourished my individual interests. I took art classes, put together my own little studio and began painting. I also began collecting found items—some were things people had left on the street for the garbage truck—and transforming them with paint or glass or bits of tile. In my own way, I made these cast-off things more *Real.* By giving them care and attention, I brought out their value. Gradually, everything around me seemed like it offered an opportunity for creative expression. In my kitchen I made a mural out of pieces of broken china. In my front hallway I stenciled swaying trees to mimic an aging fresco. In short, I began to feel happy being my *Real* self.

The self-acceptance that came with my attempt to be more *Real* made me feel less anxious and more comfortable in everyday life. It also affected the way that I viewed others. I became more patient and openhearted, and this immediately brought me closer to the people I love. This made sense. After all, if this new understanding gave me permission to be specifically myself, then I certainly had to extend the same permission to others.

As part of this change, I became much more curious about what made people think and feel the way they did. So I asked, and the answers were extremely interesting. I discovered that everyone's internal process was unique. I couldn't assume anything about anyone. Just as we know that no two snowflakes are identical, so it goes with *Real* people. The variety is endless and delightful.

If the wisdom of *The Velveteen Rabbit* had been simply a personal revelation, and nothing more, it would have been a magnificent gift. After all, the story had given me a perspective on life that had calmed years of self-criticism and doubt. But over time I came to see that the concept of being *Real* might help other people to be happier and more at peace with themselves.

As a therapist, it was my job to help clients who felt emotional pain and were struggling to function better in their personal lives, their work and their relationships. Some of the people I saw had eating disorders, obsessions, depression, anxiety and substance abuse problems. A few even practiced self-injury, cutting or burning themselves in order to stop feeling numb.

Though their symptoms varied widely, my clients expressed feelings that every one of us, if pressed, might experience at one time or another. They spoke of feeling lost, invisible and unimportant. They didn't feel accepted and loved for who they were. And they felt both grief and the nagging sense that something vital was missing. Some described a physical sensation, saying they were "empty inside" or felt "like there's a pit in my stomach."

More often than not, the talking therapy worked. People came to my office, explored both their present and past, and with my aid improved. They developed a kinder attitude—I call it self-empathy—that allowed them to look at themselves less harshly, accepting their own flaws and limitations. They also developed new faith in their own unique personalities and values. As this happened, many of the symptoms that brought them into therapy seemed to fade.

I could use psychological jargon to describe the improvement I saw, but these terms are stilted, too formal and lack the poetry to match what I was observing. A better way to describe it is: they were becoming *Real*.

Becoming *Real,* it turns out, is the purpose of every kind of psychotherapy. It is living in the moment with the deepest respect for yourself and for others. It is a way of thinking that allows us to express ourselves and experience life—including its stress, conflicts, sorrows and losses—with grace, kindness and integrity.

Why am I so certain about the power of being *Real?* First, I experienced it in my own life. Second, I saw it affect the lives of my clients. And lastly, when I introduced the concept to my students at the college where I teach courses in psychology, social work and communication, they all found it to be inspiring, easy to understand and relatively easy to incorporate in their own lives. This was more than ten years ago. And in all those years, I have yet to encounter a single person who couldn't see the value of this perspective and wasn't helped by it.

The Opposite of Real

henever you experience a big shift in your life, you begin to notice that you are different from many other people. For example, smokers who quit suddenly see how many people are still addicted. The same sort of thing happens when you give yourself permission to be *Real*. You begin to notice how many people are out of touch with their true selves.

Just a handful of my students—there have been hundreds—have felt comfortable enough to express their uniqueness in class. Most are too worried about the opinions of others—especially my opinion as their teacher—and are obsessed with the images they project. The same is true for people I have encountered in social situations. Even my close friends are sometimes anxious about appearing different from other people.

If the loss of being *Real* were all these people suffered, it would be bad enough. But there is more. Many of them had actually devoted themselves to denying, hiding and even destroying everything that made them different, special and unique. They had poured enormous amounts of energy, time and money into constructing façades they believed were more acceptable to others. They had purposely made themselves the opposite of *Real* human beings. They were *Objects*.

Obsessing about appearance is a hallmark of self-*objectification,* but it is only part of the syndrome. *Object* people worry about how others judge their jobs, their mates and their homes. They believe the cars they drive send a certain message to friends and neighbors. They prefer clothes that come from certain designers and stores. They even demand that their children act and dress in a way that reflects well on them. The mere thought of someone noticing a personal flaw, or realizing that they are simply having a problem, is a cause of constant concern.

Few of us would admit to being an *Object* person. When I first try to explain this to someone, they invariably say, "Oh, I know what you're talking about. I know someone just like that." We have trouble noticing that, at least in small and subtle ways, we have all abandoned our *Real* selves. The process of becoming an *Object* is so gradual that we don't even know it is happening.

More significantly, the powerful, *objectifying* social forces that push us to abandon our *Real* selves are so numerous, so widespread and so integrated in the landscape of our lives that we don't even notice them. They are like the air we breathe or the light that helps us see. We do not notice them unless they are called to our attention.

The United States of Generica

The social pressure that urges us to conform also makes us feel insignificant. The Velveteen Rabbit, who lived in a world where everyone was supposed to be a modern model of something flashy and new, understood that as a simple toy made of sawdust and velveteen he fell short of the ideal. Through much of Margery Williams's book, he expresses insecurity about his failure to be modern, like the other toys.

In our world, the standards used to determine a person's value generally include wealth, beauty, public acclaim, power and popularity. As a result, the most-valued people fall into a very narrowly defined group. They are all the same—generically pleasant but boring in the way they look, act and talk. They are the leading citizens of an imaginary society I call the "United States of Generica."

Like the mechanical toys in *The Velveteen Rabbit,* the citizens of the U.S. of G. embody all the latest fads and fashions. They are relatively bland in what they say, taking care to agree with the majority. They always do what is expected of them, even if that means playing the role of "bad girl" or "bad boy" of the moment. And they rarely reveal exceptional intelligence, creativity or independence.

To understand how much our culture values those who conform, consider the status of the women who pose for fashion magazines and television commercials. Top models are paid exorbitant salaries and granted more attention than Nobel Prize winners. They are given this status because they are what the word "model" means: a perfect *representation* or *imitation* of the real thing. They are joined in the ranks of the *Object* elite by athletes, who are expected to perform like machines, and pop-star celebrities, who are primped and styled to an exact, market-tested image.

Actors, athletes and models are the leading lights of the United States of Generica. Their supposed value is promoted by virtually every powerful institution in society, including the media, business, schools and families. The accepted definition of a "good life" is tilted toward unrealistic levels of perfection. At the same time, the culture makes it perfectly clear that the whole world is watching to see if we fall short of this impossible ideal. As a result, we often live in fear of the special punishment heaped on those who don't measure up: shame.

Thinglish and the Power of Shame

Although Margery Williams's Velveteen Rabbit faces many obstacles in his quest to be *Real*, few bring him more pain than the nagging sense that, in the eyes of others, he is somehow defective. Indeed, in the beginning of his tale, the Rabbit seems to have almost accepted the general wisdom of the nursery, which insists that he feel ashamed of who he is because he isn't shiny and flawless. This feeling is a terrible burden.

Few emotions are more powerful than shame. Shame breaks your bond with other people. It makes you feel rejected, alienated, isolated and alone. Shame is so unsettling that we can recall it long after the moment has passed. (This is why we all remember those times in childhood when we were ashamed.) Shame is so devastating that people will do whatever they can, almost as a reflex, to avoid it. For this reason, it is a very effective tool for enforcing the *objectifying* rules of the U.S. of G.

For example, until recently, I truly believed that my armpits were perfectly normal. Then a series of deodorant ads informed me that men really notice a beautiful, soft, smooth armpit, and they care about it enough to discuss it with each other, even admiring a woman for her stunning armpits alone. An ad like this, which sounds truly ridiculous if taken out of context, may actually cause the average woman to pause in her busy day to consider the state of her armpits and their relative desirability. I wasn't ashamed of my armpits before, but for a brief moment I wondered, *Are my armpits smooth enough? Should I buy that antiperspirant?*

When the media mouthpieces of the U.S. of G. aren't threatening you with shame, they are promising you that certain *Objects* (clothes, beer, breath mints) will make you happy. This is done with a special shaming dialect that I have come to call *"Thinglish."*

Thinglish reduces any precious and complex part of life to an *Object,* or a purchase. Using *Thinglish,* a store offers us the "good life" at a "great price," as if happiness could be purchased, and at a discount no less. A *Thinglish* bumper sticker says, "He who dies with the most toys wins." The *Thinglish* creed comes down to the statement that "You can never be too rich or too thin."

Sure, you say, that's the way they speak in advertising, but I don't really think that way. But if someone asks you to describe yourself, how would you reply? Chances are, you'd rattle off a list of your roles—"I'm a housewife, an executive, a student"—that are all generic. You are not Susan, the woman who cares so much about environmental issues that she rescues injured sea birds, volunteers with sick children in the hospital, makes handmade greeting cards and loves the color orange; instead, you are the woman who drives a crummy, old car.

Of course, it would be ridiculous to argue that *things* are inherently evil, or that commerce is bad. What I am saying is that too many of us have replaced a *Real* definition of happiness and success with one based on the acquisition of stuff and the improvement of our image. The most telling measure of this, of the effects of *objectification,* can be seen in the annual surveys of the hopes and dreams of adolescent Americans begun in the

1950s. For decades, the survey found that young people valued, above all else, a happy family life and satisfying work. The answers began to change in the 1970s, and today the two leading goals voiced by young Americans are wealth and fame, in that order.

The Price of Objectification

In *The Velveteen Rabbit,* the Skin Horse was a long-time resident of the nursery who had seen that toys who never learn the value of being *Real* invariably became victims of their own attempts to be ever more shiny and mechanically perfect. Under the pressure to excel, they fall apart and never feel the joy of being *Real.*

The same kind of fate awaits human beings who embrace the values of the U.S. of G. and forget who they *Really* are. Once we accept the pervasive messages of the *Object* culture, once we believe that we should be perfect, we start to feel shamefully inadequate. No one, after all, can ever attain the *Object* ideal. As a result, we tumble into a never-ending cycle of struggle, self-condemnation and flailing attempts to ease the pain through money, power, drugs, sex, food or purchases. You can get a good view of the dark side of the *Object* lifestyle from magazines and TV programs devoted to chronicling the lives of the rich and famous. If you pay attention to the celebrity press you will see that self-inflicted tragedies befall shiny *Object* people at a breathtaking rate. Infidelity and divorce is so common in Hollywood that a one-year wedding anniversary is regarded as a miracle. The abuse of drugs and alcohol are so widely accepted in this community that the Betty Ford Clinic is regarded as a fashionable address.

But you don't have to be a star or a mogul to suffer the downside of the *Object* life. I have seen similar problems arise in my clients' lives so often that I've come to believe that the major cause of addiction, depression, anxiety, even obsessions and compulsions, is the loss of empathy for our *Real* selves.

Just think about the process of abandoning your *Real* self. You let go of a dream here, a feeling there. Elements of yourself fall away so quietly that you don't even notice. But something inside of you feels the losses. And as the losses mount, so does the pain. I believe this feeling, this grief, is at the core of the generalized unhappiness, malaise, anxiety and depression that is epidemic in our time.

In its most extreme manifestations, *Object* thinking leads not just to grief, but also to such a complete lack of empathy that abuse, neglect, and even crime and violence become possible.

The connection between *Object* values and destructive behavior becomes plain when you consider parents who abuse their children. Parents who cannot connect with their own, human selves cannot empathize with the experiences of their sons and daughters. In this detached state, they are able to inflict shame, pain and humiliation in ways that *Real* mothers and fathers never could.

Even if you aren't facing a serious emotional or psychological crisis, you may still be covering up the grief connected to losing your *Real* self. One common side effect of being *un-Real* is to crowd your life with so many tasks, responsibilities and activities—exercise, community service, hobbies—that there's no time to feel much of anything. Being busy makes you look like the *Object* ideal. But for many of us, the hidden purpose of all this activity is to blot out feelings and produce so much distraction that we cannot see what we have lost on the road to perfection.

If an overcrowded schedule doesn't signal you that

something's wrong, you may just get a more direct message from your body. I believe that some of us feel physical pain or discomfort when we're not being *Real* about what's happening in our lives. Of course, any disturbing physical symptoms must be checked fully by your physician. But some problems—unexplained back pain is an example—can be signals of emotional distress. Stomach ailments can also fit into this category, but the classic one is the garden-variety panic attack. In many cases, these episodes, which mimic a heart attack, are linked to feelings of loss and alienation. They are signs that the repressed, *Real* self is screaming to be heard.

The damage we do to ourselves is only part of the *Object* tragedy. People who demand perfection from themselves generally start to demand it from everyone else, too. Under these conditions, it's much easier to treat members of our families, our friends and even people we meet as we move through life as things that are less than human and don't require our loving care, compassion and consideration. Like many of the characters in

The Velveteen Rabbit, we may come to believe that only people who are shiny and modern have value.

Under this paradigm, men who push themselves to be perfect *Objects* will seek women who seem to represent the idealized female, with her bland demeanor and perfect body. Then they do all they can to keep her in the *Object* role. Indeed, if something changes—say she gains weight—these men can be critical, shaming and even abusive. They cannot stand the idea of losing the *Object* they acquired because they fear it will make them look less appealing. You don't have to look far to find a case of a husband replacing his wife of his own age with a newer, younger model. One of my clients got her breasts lifted and enlarged to make herself more attractive to her husband. He was unfaithful anyway. After his cheating was discovered, he complained, "You're not the girl I married anymore!" She said, "Of course I'm not. It's twenty years later, I've grown up, and I want to be something more than an attractive accessory!"

The female equivalent may be found in wives who pressure their husbands to climb the ladder of wealth and success. One of my neighbors adopted this role, demanding that her husband change jobs and commute long distances in order to make more money. When he did what she urged him to do, she pressured him into buying a big, new expensive house, which required that he put so much time into earning the money for the mortgage he was hardly home to enjoy the place.

The man who needed a wife who never grew old, as well as the woman who tortured her husband to get the perfect house, both destroyed their marriages. Finding themselves alone, they each sank into depression, falling so low that their extended families became concerned about their very survival. *Object* living had produced for both of them the worst crisis they had ever faced. These crises also offered them a chance to get *Real*, though neither one of them could see it at first.

The Gift of a Crisis

For a stuffed bunny who lives in a nursery, the Velveteen Rabbit goes through more than his share of trials and tribulations. In the story, the Boy falls ill, and the Rabbit becomes afraid of people who would treat him as a mere thing and throw him away. In order to stay close to the Boy, and continue to support him, the Rabbit hides under the blankets. It is a frightening time, but the Rabbit's love for the Boy is stronger than his fear. Then, as the Boy recovers, the Rabbit is discarded because he is full of germs. But this rejection is not the end. The devotion and love expressed by the Velveteen Rabbit had set him on the path to becoming *Real,* and nothing will get in his way.

For those of us who wait to become *Real* human beings, the pivotal crisis is usually not caused by some outside force. Instead, it's the product of our own stubborn efforts to somehow succeed at the game of being the perfect O*bject.* Eventually, we reach a point where the sacrifices we make—the pain, trouble and conflict—are much greater than the rewards we receive for denying our true selves.

In this moment, when we feel the pain but cannot imagine doing things differently, it's easy to reach for the anesthetic of drugs, alcohol, sex and other addictions. Life spins further out of control. *Reality* seems further and further out of reach, and solutions elude us.

When I meet adults in this situation, they describe the emptiness, the emotional bankruptcy. They feel panic, self-loathing and confusion. Their relationships have no meaning, and their work feels empty. Most frightening of all, they have stopped functioning well and are terrified of being seen as unattractive and unworthy failures.

Some of my clients who reach this state have been afraid to even look for what they have lost. "I am nothing," a woman whispered to me once. "If I'm not the mother, the wife or the worker, I'm nothing."

At 'the moment of despair, when the *Object* culture has done its worst to you, it helps to remember that the Chinese symbol for crisis combines figures that depict both danger and opportunity. When you reach the point of crisis after a lifetime pursuit of the *Object* ideal, you may feel that you are in danger of losing everything— your relationships, your status, even your mind.

In fact, you face a wonderful opportunity. We are never more open to seeing the world and ourselves in a new light than when we are in crisis. When the rewards of the *Object* culture no longer work, it's easier to choose a different option, to look for the *Real* values and definitions of success that mean more to you as an individual. This always begins with a change in our beliefs about ourselves, and what is true and good.

Beliefs, Feelings, Behaviors

ventually the Velveteen Rabbit came to believe he was *Real*, and this belief spurred his trans-formation. For him, belief became *Reality*. The same can be true for us. Indeed, the connection between what we believe, what we then feel and, finally, how we behave is essential to becoming *Real*. When I discuss this chain with clients I simply write it on a piece of paper as a basic formula:

BELIEFS ⟶ FEELINGS ⟶ BEHAVIOR

Your happiness, your identity and your sense of self-worth all depend on this paradigm. Once you understand there is always this kind of flow—that your beliefs lead to feelings that prompt behaviors—you won't be quite as mystified by your actions or emotions in the same way again. It also works in understanding others in your life.

Let me give you an example. If, as I was growing up, the world around me repeated the message that smart, beautiful and highly valued women come in all different sizes, shapes and colors—even with brown hair and small breasts—I might have believed that I was a smart, beautiful and highly valued young woman. Under these circumstances, the normal obstacles of life would feel irritating, but the feeling would be transient because I would have a basic belief in my own worth. How would such a person behave? On the whole, she would behave like a pleasant, secure and even-tempered person.

On the other hand, if I grew up being told that I was stupid and ugly, my feelings and behaviors would be much different. I would feel insecure, as if the things that made me different from the ideal rendered me defective. I would be filled with self-doubt. I might be reluctant to speak up in school or in social situations for fear of calling attention to my shortcomings. And even if I became successful in life, I would be afraid that my flaws would be revealed at any moment and I would be discovered as an impostor.

The cycle of belief, feelings and behavior perpetuates and then magnifies itself. Negative beliefs cause unpleasant feelings, which make us do things that reinforce those negative beliefs. The wheel goes 'round and 'round, and before you know it, you are a discouraged person mired in a way of life that betrays your *Real* potential, intelligence, strengths and talents. Worse, you must continue to struggle to satisfy the values of the

Object society, which says that your worth is based on wealth, beauty, power and fame. Because no one can win that game, you will never feel any better.

Beliefs are learned, however, which means they can be unlearned and replaced, sort of like the way you can delete a program from a computer. Granted, *Object* beliefs are often acquired when we are very young and don't have the knowledge or ability to challenge them. But no belief is so rock solid that we cannot dislodge it later on and replace it with one that works better for us.

By now I hope you can see that *Object* thinking is profoundly damaging to ourselves as individuals, to our partners, to our children and to the communities we call home. *Objectification* destroys our empathy for our *Real* selves and for what is *Real* in others. In this state, where we lack the ability to value human beings even with their flaws and differences, it is possible to hurt people in ways that *Real* human beings cannot.

Understanding what you believe and where those beliefs came from is the key to becoming *Real*. You cannot become *Real* if you are still driven by old beliefs. You can live as a *Real* person if, like the Velveteen Rabbit, you start to believe in your heart that you are *Real*.

Choosing Empathy

I n my work with clients I don't just point people to the parable of *The Velveteen Rabbit* and say, "There is the answer to your problems." Instead, I use the story as a way to introduce serious concepts about basic beliefs, the value of the self, the way society can discourage individuality and the pain associated with being *un-Real*.

If your heart and mind are open to the Margery Williams story, you realize that it is as much a statement on the human condition as a children's book. You also become very interested in your *Real* self, including the ways that you lost touch with it and the process of finding it again.

If you quiet your mind and reflect on what you believe about yourself and your value as a person, you are likely to hear more than a few negative judgments. Some will be focused on your appearance. Others will be criticisms of your social status or even the car you drive. By now I hope you can see that these judgments are based on standards you acquired, at least in part, by simply living in the United States of Generica.

Understanding that those judgments are destructive brings us halfway to the point where we can choose new beliefs and values based on our *Real* selves. But before we can take that step, we have to care enough about ourselves to start making changes. This level of caring requires what I call self-empathy.

When we have self-empathy, we are aware of our own idiosyncratic values, priorities, needs and feelings. I'm not talking about selfishness here or narcissism. And I'm not suggesting that you place yourself above all others. Self-empathy involves tuning in to your own heart and mind as you go through each day. A person with self-empathy doesn't struggle to think what everyone else is thinking or feel what everyone else is feeling. He values his own responses and considers them when making choices and decisions.

We all enter the world with this ability. It is what stimulates babies to cry when they are uncomfortable, frightened or hungry, or to gurgle happily when they are content. (Babies don't check with each other to see if their feelings are appropriate.) But self-empathy is lost as we learn to conform and deny our individuality in order to avoid the pain of being shamed.

Self-empathy can be recovered when we begin to look at ourselves—and especially at the child we once were—with the loving eyes of an accepting adult. The experience of one of my clients, Connie, offers a good example of how this can work.

One of three children, Connie was her parents' only daughter. As is the case in many families, her mother and father had unconsciously assigned each child certain roles and personality traits. Her older brother, for example, was raised to be the family superstar. He believed this message and became both famous and wealthy in adulthood. (You would know his name if I told it here.) Connie was groomed to be a reliable, hard working and self-sacrificing daughter. She became a quiet, devoted nurse.

When I met her, Connie was in her mid-fifties and her face was fixed in a permanent frown. She dressed, spoke and acted in ways that made her invisible. Deep inside, however, Connie dreamed of a much bolder, more expansive life. She was especially drawn to travel and wanted to see the world, but she never gave herself the opportunity because she felt it would be too self-serving.

I used to tease Connie by telling her that instead of a devil on one shoulder and an angel on the other, she had a gypsy on one shoulder and Eeyore, the self-deprecating donkey from the Winnie the Pooh stories, on the other. The gypsy wanted to dance around the world. Eeyore said, "Never mind. It's all right. I don't need anything like that."

As we explored the source of Connie's beliefs about herself, she developed real empathy for the little girl she had once been. She saw how she had been molded by the culture and her family to fit a certain role and how she then fell into an inevitably muted life. This empathy made Connie care enough to change. She began to take chances and express herself. Gradually she became an avid traveler and made trips abroad that have changed her perspective on herself and her life. She's planning to go to Japan, and because she now believes in her own value, she will make it. The frown, by the way, is gone.

The magic of empathy is that as we learn to apply it to ourselves, we naturally begin to use it with others. This skill—the ability to sense and respect how someone else feels and be sensitive to their experiences—makes our relationships more authentic, more satisfying, more *Real*.

The difference between *un-Real* and *Real* relationships may be most profound in marriage and domestic partnerships. Men and women who see their partners as *Real* are not distracted by younger, firmer bodies or by people with higher status. They are taken with the very essence of the person they love, and they cannot be distracted.

Empathy can also bring dramatic changes to other relationships. Parents who empathize with children are more patient and understanding. And adults who feel true empathy for others can use it to forge *Real* relationships with older parents, even when pain clouds the past.

It is impossible to overstate the value of empathy. Empathy is behind every act of love, charity, kindness and grace. Empathy is what makes it possible for individuals, groups and even nations to coexist.

For the individual, empathy brings an ever-deepening appreciation for life's challenges and experiences. Over time, empathy helps us to respect and admire others and ourselves for having grown, adapted and survived. Scars, wrinkles, sagging flesh and other physical imperfections are merely evidence that we have lived and loved, just like the Velveteen Rabbit. Like the old woman whose husband attended her so lovingly at my doctor's office, we are loved because of our flaws, not in spite of them. In fact, they are not flaws at all. They are, instead, evidence of a lifetime of experiences.

Another major benefit of empathy is the contribution it makes to the development of human character, which is often confused with personality. In the U.S. of G. we are encouraged to develop a pleasing personality as evidenced by social skill and performance. Comedians have big personalities. So do many politicians.

But personality is often an *un-Real* thing, part of the superficial image we present in order to succeed in the world. In contrast with personality, character is dominated by our sense of ethics and our values. Good character, which leads us to acts of honesty, kindness, selflessness and courage, is only possible with empathy. It prompts creative expression of ourselves and helps us build relationships based on who we are inside, rather than external displays of wealth, status or fame. *Real* character brings us into supportive friendships, marriages and partnerships. In the end, this is what truly matters in life.

If you want proof of the great value of good character,

pay attention to people who are approaching the end of life. Few, if any of them, spend much time dwelling on the things they owned or their place in the social order. They think about whom they have loved and who has loved them for whom they *Really* are. Those with the hallmarks of good character—integrity, honesty, empathy—invariably enjoy deep, rich and varied relationships.

Principles

o one can anticipate every challenge and circumstance they will face. Life is too wonderfully complex and varied for this to be possible. But if we chose to be *Real* and pursue a life of purpose, connection to others and individuality, we can fashion some basic guidelines, some principles that help us to make decisions whenever the need arises.

By definition, a principle is a very basic and essential guide. It is a concept or ideal that can be applied to choices and competing interests. A principle is, at first glance, general and nonspecific. But it can be applied to the most specific and difficult situations we might ever face. A wonderful example is found in the physician's Hippocratic oath, which states, "Do no harm." These three simple words can guide doctors through the most harrowing situations.

The principles I explore in the next part of this book are inspired by Margery Williams's story, but draw on a host of other sources, including my own experiences and the lives of my clients. They are intended to help you to navigate the *Object* culture, to recognize what is *Real* in yourself and others, and to shape a life based on your own values, talents and character.

Over the years I have seen, time and again, that as people learn to be *Real*, they become happier and their relationships become more fulfilling. Of course, I cannot say this is the only path to love and happiness. But I do know that love and happiness bloom for people who choose a *Real* path through life. I have witnessed this transformation too many times to ignore its power.

Velveteen

Principle #1

Real Is Possible

For a long time he lived in the toy cupboard or on the nursery floor, and no one thought very much about him. He was naturally shy, and being only made of velveteen, some of the more expensive toys quite snubbed him. The mechanical toys were very superior, and looked down upon everyone else; they were full of modern ideas and pretended they were real.

The plot of Margery Williams's book revolves around the Velveteen Rabbit's quest to become *Real* and resolve his doubts about his own identity and worth. The promise of this sweet story is fulfilled when the Rabbit finally realizes that he has achieved his goal and becomes a real rabbit made of flesh and blood. He jumps and whirls about because he has been freed from his feelings of failure and inadequacy.

However, a sensitive reader—and all children are

sensitive readers—notices that the little Rabbit begins to show signs of being *Real* from the moment that he learns that such a thing is possible. The essence of what is *Real*—kindness, empathy and individuality—is already inside the Rabbit. It was born in him. But the pressure of living among toys who value only mechanical perfection and the most modern ideas—the way people prize technology and follow momentary fads—had made him insecure. It would take some time for him to feel secure and completely comfortable just being himself. But the process was helped by the love he received as he allowed himself to be ever more honest about who he *Really* was on the inside.

The same basic truth—that what is *Real* waits inside—applies to all of us. You can see this truth in very young children. Look at the artwork they produce. Listen to the stories they tell. Watch how they relate to each other. Unless a young child has been purposely inhibited or silenced, she will show you a remarkably individual spirit. She is *Real*.

Sadly, most of us lose touch with this spirit as we move through life and come under the influence of the *Object* culture. Society's one-size-fits-all recipe for success disconnects us from what is *Real*. It forces us into roles that ignore our individuality and require us to reject what is *Real* in other people. Many of us adopt a mask of conformity, which we wear as we move through a world in which everyone else wears a mask, too.

This disconnection from what is *Real* may be most evident in the world of work, which sometimes dominates our adult lives. Many of us have trouble finding jobs that allow us to express our true values and talents. Early in Williams's book, for example, the Velveteen Rabbit's most wonderful quality—he was what my daughters would have called a wonderful "hugger" toy—was completely overlooked.

The fact that so many of us cannot be ourselves at work may be why a great many of my clients spend a lot of time talking about their jobs. Work is a place where many people feel disappointed, empty and unfulfilled, even though they are supposed to feel successful. I can relate to this experience because I once lost touch with my *Real* self when I took a job that everyone else considered a plum.

When I finished my undergraduate degree in theater, I followed the path that my training had established, working first for a small public television station doing production and some on-air work, and then moving on to a top-rated commercial affiliate in a big East Coast city. Although I was interested in making quality programs aimed at children, I quickly learned that life at the station was organized around something else—a competition for promotions, raises and recognition. Those who won the competition *might* get the chance to do meaningful television.

After six months of dressing for success (translation: sexy and uncomfortable) and spending my days in corporate combat, I felt exhausted, unmotivated and downright depressed. As I thought about how I spent my days, I realized that my job did not call for the use of any of my creative skills. I wasn't valued for my unique potential and contributions. I was a cog in a large machine, a part that could be readily replaced.

Any clear-minded person with a *Real* approach to life would have recognized that the pain I felt at the time was a result of the clash between my true desires, hopes and dreams and the situation I encountered at work. It was a signal that I had lost touch with what was *Real* about me.

But because I had accepted the idea that my job in the supposedly glamorous world of television gave me some sort of status, I was reluctant to change. In fact, I felt both guilty and like a failure because I wasn't enjoying it. It would take almost another year of confusion for me to realize that I didn't fit the job or, to put it more *Realistically,* the job didn't fit me.

Eventually the pain of being *un-Real* made me quit, and I began a long process of soul-searching and reflection. I realized that I had not chosen a type of work that satisfied the *Real* me. I was intensely interested in how people develop and grow, and how they recover from psychological trauma and pain. Ignoring friends and relatives who said it was a bad idea, I went back to school and became a psychotherapist.

In my practice I encounter a great many people who have lost track of their *Real* talents, desires and passions. Many of these same people blame their depression, anxiety, substance abuse and other symptoms on their jobs. They have a bad boss. They dislike their coworkers. They are underpaid.

In a way, people are right to put some of the blame for how they feel on their jobs. But the critical element in their analysis is not their boss, their coworkers or their salaries.

The big issue, and the true source of their pain, is the very problem I had when I worked in television. I had bought into society's definition of success, and thus lost touch with my *Real* self. My confusion had been a sign of the great conflict between my individual talents and interests and the job I had chosen at that big-time TV station.

Although people may feel more comfortable talking about their frustrations with work, a second area of life is an equally powerful source of inner conflict: parenting. To be more specific, with a little effort I can usually help any mother who comes into my office express her rarely voiced fear that she is not living up to the cultural ideal.

No role in life, as presented by the media and other influential institutions, is more impossible to play than that of mother. Women with children are expected to know everything about health, child development, home-making, education, values and more. They are also expected to guide their children with absolutely flawless judgment, while making sure they are the smartest, strongest, most excellent kids who ever walked the Earth.

I'm not finished. Besides being a perfect teacher and nurturer, today's moms are also supposed to be super-efficient money managers who get their kids the best, newest and latest without putting a strain on the family budget. And it doesn't hurt, according to the U.S. of G., if this same woman becomes a perfectly energized and sexy woman the moment the kids are put to bed at night.

With all the TV programs, magazine articles, friends, neighbors and relatives telling America's mothers what they should do, is it any wonder that so many lose touch with their individuality? Of course, what every child truly needs is a mother whose unique love, guidance and caring flow from inside. The trouble is, nobody encourages mothers (or fathers for that matter) to take this less-traveled road.

It may seem strange to focus on parenting and work at the start of a book that encourages you to be a *Real* individual guided by your own talents, interests and idiosyncrasies. Maybe you expected me to address something more esoteric and less practical.

However, I have discovered that when I first introduce the topic of being *Real*, most people see my point—and how they have lost touch with their *Real* selves—if I use examples related to work and family life. Both are down-to-earth propositions.

When people talk about their problems in these areas of life, they often begin complaining about superficial things. But when we go deeper, we begin to discuss issues that touch on their individual personalities, character and emotions. People say they feel unimportant, powerless, bored and like they are wasting their time.

One man told me, "I'm like a cartoon character sitting around watching dials and eating donuts. I do my job so I can pay my bills, that's it." A similar tone emerges when mothers talk about how they struggle to keep up with society's expectations. They become "mommy machines" rushing around, doing tasks they fear add nothing of substance to their own lives or to their children's lives. I understand how they feel. We all want to use our talents and time in a way that is challenging and produces something of value for others. In short, we want our work to match our *Real* dreams.

One of the most fascinating truths that emerges in most of my sessions with people who are unhappy with their roles as workers or parents is that money and status don't matter as much as they once thought. Indeed, once they start exploring their choices and trying to figure out how they lost touch with their *Real* interests and values, many see that they were pushed off course by society's expectations. A mother I know succumbed to an endless round of carpooling to various after-school activities because everyone else was doing it. A friend of mine never followed his dream of teaching music because he kept accepting promotions from a grocery store chain where he started as a summer employee.

No one should blame himself or herself for landing in a spot that doesn't feel *Real*. The entire economy is organized to drive people to be compliant. Teachers, parents, friends and neighbors all expect us to fall into line, and they promise rewards that cannot be achieved. At my TV job I was told that I would be able to produce positive programs that would educate viewers. That was never going to happen, but I needed more than a year to figure it out.

When they begin to realize that they've devoted themselves to false ideals, a lot of people get lost in blaming themselves. Not only is this a waste of time, it's a bad analysis. With so many powerful cultural forces pushing you to conform, how much control did you have? Very few people can ignore the pressure and follow only their *Real* interests. Most of us have to feel the pain that comes from being a square peg in a round hole before we even begin to consider that something might be wrong.

Once you understand that the key to a more satisfying and *Real* life waits inside you, the transformation has already started. Like the Velveteen Rabbit, who began to become *Real* the moment he discovered that such a thing was possible, we all take a giant step toward *Reality* the first time we decide that we want to rediscover our individual values, passions and hopes. It doesn't matter if the first aspect of life you chose to examine is work. All that matters is that you have begun.

We can make progress toward a more fulfilling life if we adopt what I call, rather ironically, a *Realistic* point of view. In the way most people use the term, being realistic means settling for what you can get. But in my view, we are realistic when we honor our special abilities, interests and dreams. These all come from our deep, *Real* selves.

Maybe your *Real* self needs close contact with other people, the kind that comes from being a health-care provider or teacher. Perhaps you need the satisfaction of creating something from scratch, the way craftsmen and artists do. Or maybe you enjoy the challenge of organizing people to tackle a complex problem, like the creation of a new business or community organization. The satisfaction you feel if you allow yourself to pursue these *Real* needs and interests will make you much happier than any number of zeroes on your paycheck.

A *Real* life is possible for each one of us. Although Margery Williams never spells it out, her little Velveteen Rabbit takes the same route to being *Real* that we all must follow. He discovers the value of being *Real*, explores what is in his heart, and takes time to develop all of the qualities he will need, from courage to generosity, in order to live by his own design.

If you ever lose faith in this process, or doubt your ability to make yourself *Real*, remember that from the very moment he realized that he wanted to be *Real*, the

Velveteen Rabbit was making it happen. And the rewards make the struggle worthwhile. Just consider how the Velveteen Rabbit felt when he finally understood that he was *Real*.

. . . He gave one leap and the joy of using those hind legs was so great that he went springing about the turf on them, jumping sideways and whirling around as the others did. . . . He was a Real Rabbit, at last. . . .

Velveteen

Principle #2

Real Is a Process

"Does it happen all at once, like being wound up," he asked, "or bit by bit?" "It doesn't happen all at once," said the Skin Horse. "You become. It takes a long time. That's why it doesn't often happen to people who break easily, or have sharp edges, or have to be carefully kept."

In Margery Williams's story, the oldest and wisest resident of the nursery is the Skin Horse, a stuffed animal that has been loved so long and so hard that all of his hair has been rubbed off. The Velveteen Rabbit, a new arrival, recognizes that the Skin Horse is happy, content and secure in a way the other toys are not. He decides that he wants to be content, too, and he becomes intensely curious about how that might happen.

In the little society that exists in the nursery, the windup toys create instant gratification when their gears start turning. As they move and make noise, they put on impressive displays for everyone to see. But the excitement passes quickly, and they must be wound up again and again to keep up the charade. We all know what happens soon enough. Springs break. Gears jam. Wheels fall off.

The same things happen to us when we depend on momentary achievements and the things we can buy to give us a sense of self-worth. The *Object* culture tells us that the frenzied pursuit of stuff and status will make us feel better. And for a while it may work. But the lift provided by major purchases or career advancements is almost always short-lived. So we set our sights on another purchase or another achievement and start chasing it. The process can be endless. It is the trap that snares us when we think of life as a series of goals.

In contrast, the Skin Horse says *Real* is something you *become* over time. It is the process of discovering and defining yourself and then cultivating a life that fits those defining qualities. I believe you start to become *Real* as soon as this process begins and that you can become ever more *Real* as you grow and mature and keep refining what matters most to you.

"Okay," you might say, "I understand that certain basic human needs and desires are part of living *Real*. But what are they?"

Although it's essential that we all embrace our own

idiosyncratic priorities, there are some aspects of being *Real* that everyone seems to need. As you start the process of identifying your core values, you might keep these general themes in mind.

Close relationships make us feel more *Real.* Human beings are social animals. Close, safe relationships make us feel happy and secure. Of course, these relationships can only be *Real* when we are honest about ourselves and our feelings.

Work that matters makes us feel more *Real.* Work that matters involves something more than making money. It contributes something worthwhile to other people and has a positive effect on your community. This doesn't mean we all have to be social workers or volunteers. But if your job doesn't allow you to feel like you're providing a fair and honest service or product, then it won't make you feel *Real.*

Creativity and growth make us feel *Real.* Whenever we learn something new, try something new or create something new, we feel more *Real.* Again, I'm not talking about something fancy like oil painting or sculpture. People express themselves in a million ways, and we grow when we take a walk with a loved one, work in the garden with a grandchild or just read a book.

Teaching, nurturing and caring for others make us feel *Real*. New parents always say that the arrival of a child changed them completely. What they usually mean is that it allowed them to step out of themselves and give wholeheartedly to another person. You don't have to be a mother or father to do this. Opportunities to teach, nurture and care are everywhere.

These four basic categories are just the beginning. You could think of many more, and you certainly could put your own spin on the ones listed above. The key thing to notice is that none of them relate to something you can buy or something you achieve once and then set aside. Relationships, work, creative activities and giving to others—these are all processes. They are ways of being, and they keep us *Real*.

While the *Object* culture stresses instant gratification, the best science, philosophy and theology support the idea that a satisfying life occurs in the long process of establishing and maintaining relationships, talents, meaningful work and service to others. This is why the philosopher Kierkegaard wrote, "Life is not a problem to be solved but a reality to be experienced." It is what writer Thomas La Mance meant when he coined the popular phrase, "Life is what happens to us when we are making other plans."

But we don't need to depend on great thinkers to show us that it is the journey, not the destination, that matters most. I am sure that in your own life you have experienced this truth. It comes up often in my work with therapy clients. One mother I see fretted for months over her daughter's moods, but failed every time she tried to interrogate her daughter about what was going on. Then she decided to devote a long, un-structured afternoon to her daughter. They had a nice lunch together and went for walk on a beach. Halfway through the afternoon, her daughter started talking about her life and let her mother know what was really bothering her. It only happened because her mother let herself enjoy an afternoon with her daughter and let go of pursuing the goal of getting to the bottom of things.

The experience of that mother and daughter shows what happens when you allow life to flow as a process. They became close because they allowed themselves to be *Real* and relax together. They valued the time together, not what might be achieved.

The connection that the mother and daughter created in their time together is a hallmark of being *Real*, and it illustrates one big difference between a life seen as a never-ending series of achievements and acquisitions and a *Real* life that is a constantly evolving process. In one, people may experience a great deal of short-term excitement and fun. In the other, they find true happiness.

What is the difference between happiness and fun? To answer this question let me tell you about a very anxiety-prone man who had trouble relating to his teenage son. For years the father struggled and failed to get his son to join in taking care of their house and yard. But when he decided that the family needed a backyard shed, he asked his son to be a partner in the project. They searched the Internet together to find a shed that came in a kit. Then, when it arrived, they set aside a weekend to put it together.

A hundred times before, this man and his son had argued over the simplest chores. But this shed project was like an enormous picture puzzle, one they had picked out together, and they quickly fell into a comfortable rhythm of working at it. When I saw the father the next week, he said they had so much fun that they were both sorry when the job was finished. Then he stopped to correct himself. What he had experienced wasn't simply fun. It was *Real* happiness, and he will cherish the experience long after the shed is gone.

Of course we all want to have fun, and there's nothing wrong with that. But if you are having lots of fun and still feel unsatisfied and empty, reflect on the differences between these two words. Fun is generic. A roller-coaster ride, for example, is fun in the same way for everyone. But it cannot make you happy unless it is shared with someone, and you feel closer from having that time together. A better example might be seen when a parent and child play catch in the backyard. The game is fun, but being together—chatting between throws, laughing at your errors—makes you happy.

One other note about happiness as a process: Sometimes finding happiness involves delaying gratification and forgetting fun for a while. Think of those driver's-ed classes you took in order to get your license. They weren't fun, but the independence you experienced when you first got behind the wheel probably made you happy.

You will notice in the examples I cite, and in your own experience, that being *Real* and engaging in the process requires one important quality—patience. The Skin Horse makes it very clear that "it takes a long time" to become *Real*. On the following page the Velveteen Rabbit responds the way most of us would. He heaves a big sigh. But he also shows remarkable resilience and patience as he evolves into a *Real* rabbit.

In contrast with the nursery in *The Velveteen Rabbit,* we live in a world where everything happens quickly. Every day brings a scientific breakthrough or an advance in technology that helps us move a little faster. But we don't exploit these advances by taking more time to think and reflect. Instead, we push ourselves harder. Perhaps the best example of this is the businessperson who saves days' worth of travel time by taking an airplane coast-to-coast. Instead of using the time on the plane to relax, she'll work on her computer. When she lands, she pulls out a cell phone to call the office.

In this frantic world, the idea that we might have to wait to get something important can sound foreign and even disturbing. We may even start to feel bad about ourselves, as if we should be able to do everything quickly and perfectly the first time. But there is no shortcut when it comes to being *Real*. The process is a long-term endeavor. It requires you to share the precious gift of time—and yourself—with the faith that you will experience *Real* happiness along the way.

If you doubt that you are capable of the deliberate thought and commitment of time that it might take to be *Real*, remember that today's high-speed lifestyle is a recent and somewhat false construct. Human beings are not hyperactive by nature. For most of time, people lived according to the seasons, not the clock, and the old were revered for how they had grown and developed over a lifetime. You can become more patient, with yourself and others. As you do, you will find that the process of becoming *Real* offers its own deep rewards every day.

Velveteen

Principle #3

Real Is Emotional

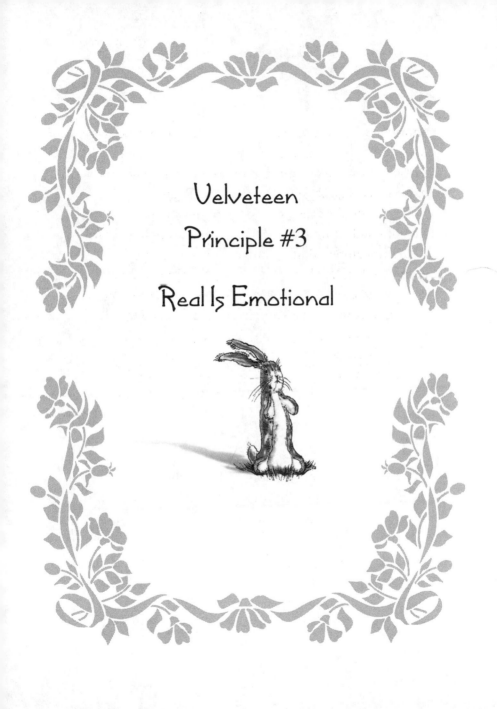

That night, and for many nights after, the Velveteen Rabbit slept in the Boy's bed. At first he found it rather uncomfortable, for the Boy hugged him very tight, and he sometimes pushed him so far under the pillow that the Rabbit could scarcely breathe. . . . But very soon he grew to like it, for the Boy used to talk to him, and made nice tunnels for him under the bedclothes that he said were like the burrows the real rabbits lived in.

Feelings play a big role in the story of *The Velveteen Rabbit*. At various points the Rabbit feels insecure, impatient, frightened and loving. And from the start of the book right through to the end, he expresses a constant and intense emotional longing to be as *Real* as the Skin Horse.

The horse, for his part, makes it very clear that the process of becoming *Real* depends on understanding, acknowledging and expressing our true emotions. In the story, the Rabbit honestly admits to his discomfort. His ability to do this without denying his feelings frees him to also experience the love and attention the Boy is offering.

When we are *Real* we are honest about how we feel. We behave in a way that is authentic and sensitive to our emotions, and we respect what our feelings tell us. This is not because emotions are superior to reason. We need both. However, our feelings do give us the truest and most immediate feedback possible about many situations. They flash early warning signals in times of danger and reliable green lights when we encounter something or someone good.

For some people, this view of human emotions can be hard to accept, but don't take my word for it. Scientists studying the brain in action have seen that in many situations our feelings—pleasure, caution, delight, fear—signal important information much faster than the rational, reasoning parts of our brains ever could. In fact, feelings are shortcuts that the mind, especially that *Real* part of the mind, uses to snap us to attention.

A good example of an emotional shortcut is the hollow

feeling you get in the pit of your stomach—one of my students calls it the "belly barometer"—when someone asks you to go against your own moral code. This is your *Real* self sending your conscious mind a clear warning.

The problem for many of us is that we are numbed to or ignore our own emotions. The feelings are there. We cannot shut them off. They will always influence how we behave. But we are often unaware of this. We lack the ability to recognize or notice our emotions, or else we paste very general labels onto our feelings, believing everything we experience can be boiled down to a few simple moods.

I see this all the time when I'm working with married couples. Often a woman will say, "I feel sad," or "I'm hurt," in response to most situations. "Sad" and "hurt" are culturally acceptable emotions for women, while anger, vengefulness and other more strident feelings are considered unladylike and shameful. Many men, on the other hand, will announce that they feel "really angry" about every disturbing thing that happens, even if it seems to me that fear, shame or confusion would be more appropriate. "Angry" is okay for men. "Afraid" is not.

How do so many of us lose touch with our emotional experiences and the vocabulary to describe them? The process usually begins early in life, when children are punished for expressing themselves in ways that make adults uncomfortable and rewarded for stifling or denying their true feelings.

This is done in a variety of ways. We give a crying kid a cookie, but ignore what she is crying about. Or we laugh at an exuberant little boy and make him feel embarrassed to show joy. Feelings can even be killed with nothing more than a look. One of my clients recalls that when he was a child and something made him begin to cry, his mother looked at him like he was "rancid meat." This always stopped his tears. On the other hand, whenever he endured real pain without complaint, like the time he broke his arm and didn't cry, he was praised as a "good little soldier."

Of course, no matter how stifling a family may be, certain feelings are permitted, especially if they conform to rigid concepts of gender. Girls are often granted a little more leeway when it comes to emotion. They are expected to express themselves more openly. But they also live under pressure to conform to certain stereotypes. Aggression, pride and ambition are often regarded as inappropriate for female children. Boys can show anger, happiness and determination, but they better not exhibit fear, anxiety or too much compassion.

Don't get me wrong. It is not acceptable for kids to be impulsive or completely unrestrained when they go out into the world. The trouble is, most adults don't see the line between self-control and self-denial. If we suppress a child's feelings to the point where they seem to vanish, he will become an adult who is so disconnected from his feelings that he can no longer count on them to support his *Real* priorities and values. Without the guidance of his feelings, he's likely to make all sorts of choices—in his career, family life, friendships—that will lead to unhappiness.

Even if we learn to suppress all our feelings, they never disappear completely. They are there, and deep down we know it. And the longer we try to hide them away, the more powerful they seem to be. Often, when I meet people who live in this state of emotional paralysis, they are downright afraid to look inside their hearts because they are afraid of what they might find.

The truth is that we all experience troubling and even

unattractive emotions like greed, envy and even rage. No matter how hard we try to deny them, they are still there. There is nothing shameful about them. The trouble occurs when we are unable to put these feelings in the proper perspective, one that accepts them as *Real* but within our control. To do so, we must allow ourselves to experience and acknowledge them.

If we don't acknowledge and accept our emotions, they are bound to leak out anyway, when we least expect it. It happens when we are inexplicably impatient with a spouse, critical of a child or simply snotty to a sales-clerk. These mysterious, cranky episodes are often the product of a suppressed feeling that we didn't acknowledge and try to understand in the moment it arose. Feelings have their own energy. We may think we had it licked when we ignored it, but pushing it aside almost never works.

Fortunately, the emotional centers in the brain never really stop working. We just stop noticing what they're trying to tell us. No matter how long and hard you have worked to suppress your feelings, everyone has the capacity to develop a more accurate sense of his or her own emotions. It's a process of slowly excavating yourself. I often start people on the path to *Reality* by handing them a printed list of the feelings they may experience day in and day out without even noticing. It includes dozens and dozens of words for their inner experiences.

abandoned	empty	loving
abused	excited	manic
aggravated	exuberant	miserable
angry	failing	nauseous
anxious	fragile	nervous
aroused	frustrated	numb
ashamed	grandiose	open
attractive	grateful	overwhelmed
blank	happy	pained
bored	helpful	perplexed
childlike	helpless	powerless
clean	hopeful	quiet
cold	hopeless	restless
comfortable	horrified	sad
confused	impatient	sedated
creative	incompetent	sexy
dependent	inconsolable	stingy
depressed	independent	suspicious
determined	insecure	thrilled
dirty	irritable	tired
disconnected	itchy	uncomfortable
distracted	jealous	violent
distraught	jumpy	vulnerable
dizzy	lazy	wise
drained	lethargic	wistful
elated	lost	withdrawn

Once people see my list of feelings, they understand the breadth, complexity and variety of human emotions. Many are so tickled by this realization they'll add new words and definitions to my collection. They see that the list is only the beginning. After you understand this, the next step is to begin listening to your own emotions.

This sensitivity, which I call self-empathy, is the one emotional tool that is critical to leaving the *Object* life behind and becoming *Real*. It's a kind of self-awareness that many people lack because they disconnect from their own experiences. Oftentimes they have to guess at their own responses, as though they are separate from themselves. But with the feelings list in hand, most people can eventually describe how they feel at that moment. Many come up with three or four words that label their emotional state. And they are genuinely surprised to notice how much is going on inside of them when they thought nothing was happening at all.

The next step is to begin living with the list. Get a small notebook and carry it and the list with you. Every hour or so, stop and consult the list and record your feelings. Then compare how you feel with how you are acting. The results can be startling. One woman I work with wrote the words "anxious, depressed, helpless and hopeless" during an afternoon visit with her in-laws. She then struggled to hide those feelings, even from herself. Later that night she ate an entire box of cookies. When we got together a few days later she was able to see that those buried feelings were related to her evening binge. Indeed, a whole lifetime of binging was connected to feelings she had steadfastly denied. Food, after all, is an *Object*, and you cannot solve an emotional problem with a *thing*.

It took a while, but my binge-eating client eventually put her pattern of denial and eating into a *Realistic* perspective. She arranged with her husband to limit her contact with the in-laws. When she was with them she avoided difficult topics of discussion. After visits she talked about her feelings, and she didn't feel the same urge to soothe herself with food.

Although it might feel artificial and difficult at first, it doesn't take long for emotional self-empathy to become a habit. And if it seems self-indulgent to focus so intently on your own feelings, consider the end point:

empathy for others. It happens every time. As people learn to recognize and respect their own feelings, they begin to do the same with others. Gradually they learn to respect and appreciate the feelings and idiosyncrasies of lovers, friends, children and others.

Becoming emotionally sensitive does have its side effects. With family and friends you might discover you have strong reactions to what is said, and what isn't said, in the kinds of conversations that once seemed innocuous. You will eventually learn to manage these feelings and how you respond to them. In the meantime, you will experience authentic empathy for yourself and everyone else. Sure, it makes life a little more complicated, but it's also much richer and more *Real* when you can feel what's going on.

As you become more empathetic, you are also likely to feel happier and more connected to others. This is because emotion and empathy are essential elements of human nature. Anthropologists have long argued that humans would never have survived if they didn't develop the empathy needed to work together, care for each other and form attachments. Indeed, it was those who did this the best who survived to pass along their genes. That's why it feels good, deep inside, to honor your feelings and the feelings of others. It's only human.

Velveteen

Principle #4

Real Is Empathetic

The mechanical toys were very superior, and they looked down upon everyone else. Between them all the poor little Rabbit was made to feel very insignificant and common-place and the only person who was kind to him at all was the Skin Horse.

When you are not *Real*, it's nearly impossible to relate to others with patience and understanding. In Margery Williams's story, Timothy the wooden soldier and all the other mechanical toys seem unable to express kindness. Williams hints at one reason. She notes that the self-important model boat has lost "most of his paint." His insecurity and fear of being seen as less than perfect lay behind his façade of superiority. He couldn't show empathy for others when he was secretly ashamed of himself.

In contrast, the Skin Horse is *Really* honest and not ashamed of his imperfect self. When we are like this, it gets much easier to embrace other people as they are. The Skin Horse was so *Real* that it was easy, second nature actually, for him to recognize the beauty and value in the Rabbit. He readily empathized with the lonely, bashful newcomer and was kind to him from the beginning.

When we have empathy, we understand that people are, at their core, emotional beings and that their feelings are affected by every experience they may have. We also know that another person's emotional response to a given situation may not be the same as our own, and we are very interested in knowing their true feelings.

Empathy is different from sympathy, which is actually defined as "agreement." When we say we sympathize with someone, we join with them. Empathy does not require joining or blending yourself emotionally with another person. It is more a matter of caring, inquiring and understanding. It can be practiced whenever we are with others, and it helps us to learn and appreciate the limitless varieties of human experience. Empathy makes it possible for us to see the goodness, beauty and positive intent being expressed all around us. Often these wonderful qualities are present in situations we would have once found maddening or frustrating.

To see how empathy works, it helps to look at an

ordinary situation where the *absence* of empathy led to a tear in a relationship, but the use of empathy repaired it. In this case, I was working with a young couple, Jan and Steven, who were expecting their first baby in a month or so. When they arrived at my office, they both seemed annoyed and confused. The object of their turmoil, at least on the surface, was a box of crullers.

As the mom-to-be explained it, on a recent rainy night she had developed a powerful craving for donuts. Pregnancy being what it is, Jan had trouble getting donuts off her mind. Eventually she spoke up, and Steven volunteered to brave the elements and satisfy her hunger.

The trouble began when Steven got to the store. They were all out of donuts. The closest thing he could find was a box of crullers. Donuts and crullers are made from the same stuff and cooked in the same way, and so he figured they were close enough. But when he got back home, soaked and cold, he didn't get the hero's welcome he expected.

"The minute I saw the crullers I felt like he hadn't listened to me at all—again!" recalled Jan, as she sat on the sofa in my office. Jan had been feeling anxious and self-conscious about her pregnancy and had been looking to Steven for support. For weeks she had been feeling disappointed, like he didn't care enough about her. The crullers were the last straw, the ultimate illustration of how he had failed to fully support her.

Steven, who felt he had demonstrated his concern for Jan by going out in the rain, and who truly believed that a cruller is a donut by another name, was at first flabbergasted and then angered by the reception he received. Some of what he said, especially about Jan being "ridiculous," clearly hurt her feelings.

Although it may seem silly to pour an entire hour of counseling into this topic, that is exactly what we did. We began by agreeing that "it wasn't about the donuts," but rather about how Jan and Steven were feeling about themselves, the pregnancy and the ways their lives would change when the baby arrived. For months Jan had been feeling more and more like a pregnancy *Object,* and less like herself. She was worried about how Steven and everyone else saw her, and she was frightened about the future. Steven was anxious about whether he could help Jan through the pregnancy and delivery. He was afraid that he would fail as a father and that the good things about his life with Jan would be overwhelmed by their new roles as parents.

As Jan and Steven talked, I could see the effect of

their honesty. As each of them admitted to fears and anxieties, their faces got brighter and their voices sounded lighter. Understanding that their worries were normal, Jan and Steven began interacting in a more direct and caring way. Steven let Jan know he thought she was still the most beautiful person in the world and that the future would be happy. Jan, feeling empathy for Steven, said that just having him stand by her would be enough to see her through to delivery. And as for his future as a father, she said, "I knew you would be a good father before we even got married."

Once they got talking about their feelings in an honest, courageous, *Real* way, Jan and Steven felt empathy for each other. They also began to use one of the best techniques available to anyone who wants to understand others and feel true empathy. They separated another person's *intent* from the *outcome* in a given situation.

Whenever we struggle to comprehend another person's behavior, especially when we feel hurt by someone we love, the key to understanding lies in that person's intent, not the outcome. Steven *intended* to do something nice for Jan. He *intended* to satisfy her craving and show his concern. The *outcome* of his efforts—crullers not donuts—was not exactly what Jan had hoped to get. But if she had focused on his *intent,* then she could have felt good about him.

The intent-versus-outcome test works in a great many circumstances because in *Real* life—meaning our life with those we love and care for—people typically do not set out to hurt us. Of course, good intentions do not erase the damage some people inflict when they are careless, take unnecessary risks or make bad choices. A teenager who bangs up the family car because he wasn't careful needs to hear about doing better next time. But if you believe that he fully intended to drive responsibly, you can have some empathy. More important, you won't react in a way that might leave lasting damage on your relationship.

Here's a useful tool if you are a parent: If you want to know whether you parent with *Real* empathy that recognizes a child as an individual, consider whether you use a lot of *Thinglish* parenting language. Statements like "Because I'm the mommy, that's why," or "I don't have to explain myself to you," are pure *Thinglish.* They remind your child, in an unnecessary way, that you hold the power. These are dead-end, conversation-killing statements. They teach kids that their parents don't want to hear their point of view. And often, in response, children act out more aggressively to get the parents to see them as specific individuals. This almost always backfires, with the rift growing ever wider with each misunderstanding and lost opportunity.

Empathetic communication happens as we speak from the heart in a way others can grasp. Consider the model boat in *The Velveteen Rabbit* who ". . . never missed an opportunity of referring to his rigging in technical terms." This is pure *Thinglish*—and the exact wrong way to speak to anyone.

Of course, more important than the way we speak is the way we listen. Empathetic listeners always tune into another person's point of view. This means that when we ask a question—even a simple, pass-the-time kind of question like "How are you?"—we are sincerely curious about the answer.

This sounds obvious, but think about the last few

phone calls you answered. Didn't almost all of the callers ask, in a perfunctory way, "How are you?" Did they sound like they wanted a truthful answer? If they didn't, it may have been because they were rushed for time and couldn't wait for a genuine response. In this case, I think, it's better that we don't ask. People know, on a gut level, whether you care to hear what they have to say. It's better to be honest about being in a hurry than to feign interest.

This is why it's never a good idea to begin formulating a response before the person you are listening to stops talking. For one thing, other people can sense that your mind is drifting, and you are not paying full attention. For another, you can't possibly reply to the true content of someone's statement before you have heard all of it. So unless you're on a game show, listen to the complete message before you respond.

Conversations may also go off track when someone has a hidden agenda. This often happens when we set aside time to be with someone—say, over lunch—and pretend it's a casual get-together when we actually have an important topic to discuss.

You have probably been in this situation with a family member. She asks to meet for coffee. After a little chitchat, which makes you relax, comes a torrent of questions and requests. You feel ambushed.

Hidden agendas destroy relationships because they practically announce out loud that you do not have empathy for another person. How can this be handled better?

Be honest about your interests. Don't hide the purpose of the conversation. This doesn't mean dispensing with manners and social niceties. You can still be friendly. But don't lie about your intentions.

I recognize there are many times when empathy won't be a significant part of our dealings with others. There are very few business meetings, for example, that offer us an opportunity to be *Real*. But we can maximize the number of *Real* encounters we enjoy each day and increase the level of empathy we bring to them.

When we are able to put ourselves in another's place, trying to understand their experience and feelings, it's possible to interpret their actions and choices in the most positive and generous way.

Every day gives us opportunities to put this perspective to work. Consider, for instance, when you get stuck on the road behind an elderly driver. He drives at a snail's pace, steers with wobbly imprecision, and leaves his turn signal on for miles at a stretch. After enduring just a few minutes behind this kind of driver, many of us feel frustrated, even angry. I've heard people say things like, "You're old, accept it, and get out of my way!"

But if we want to approach the issue of unsteady older drivers with a conscious desire to empathize, we must begin by considering their intent. Is that older driver trying to annoy us deliberately? Does he truly *want* to slow down traffic? Does he hope to confuse us by keeping his turn signal on?

An empathetic attitude would have us look for the most positive way to think about those older drivers on the road. Think about the senior motorists as individuals, with their own desires, fears, hopes and dreams. It doesn't take much effort to realize that many are still safe drivers and that operating a car for them represents autonomy, self-respect and vitality. Driving keeps them in touch with friends. It allows them to go to work and take care of their own needs independently. Giving it up would feel like an indignity, and it would hurry a not-so-pleasant confrontation with mortality.

With an empathetic frame of mind, your whole approach

to elderly drivers changes in ways that benefits them and you. They get to drive without hearing the sound of your car horn, which could upset or frighten them. You enjoy a quiet moment admiring their gumption, and perhaps you'll set an example that will influence others to have patience in the future when you are a senior driver.

Ultimately, your empathy can make your own experience better. And because everything we do can ripple into the world, affecting others, it may even make the world a better place for all of us to navigate, no matter our age.

Velveteen

Principle #5

Real Is Courageous

The little Rabbit lay among the old picture-books in the corner of the fowl house and he felt very lonely. . . . Of what use was it to be loved and lose one's beauty and become Real if it all ended like this? And a tear, a real tear, trickled down his little shabby velvet nose and fell to the ground.

One of the more surprising and inspiring elements of *The Velveteen Rabbit* story is the Rabbit's courage. At several points in the tale, he is mocked, abandoned, rejected and discouraged. There are times when he cries and almost gives up on his goal, but he somehow finds the courage to go on. It is in these moments that something truly extraordinary happens—a toy bunny cries a *Real* tear.

For those of us who live outside the pages of a children's book, becoming *Real* requires us to be brave as we change some of our priorities and present our new selves to friends, loved ones and colleagues.

There's a very good chance that after reading the previous paragraph you thought, "Well, this is where I get off. I'm a wimp. If being *Real* is about never being afraid, then I can't do it."

Relax. Being *Real* doesn't require you to live without fear. People who claim they are never afraid are just kidding themselves. And admitting that we have fears, along with every other basic human trait, is just another part of being *Real*. After all, the Velveteen Rabbit's most powerful moment of transformation—the moment when he actually becomes *Real*—involves tears, fears and despair.

What you must understand is that while a lot of things scare us, we cannot let them run our lives. Fears are more powerful when we struggle to deny them. If you acknowledge your fears and incorporate them in your sense of self, you will find it much easier to move forward, despite them. That is a *Real* definition of bravery—moving forward, even when we are afraid.

One of the most universal human fears is the one we feel when we believe we are about to be isolated or rejected. It would make sense for this feeling to arise as we begin to assert our individuality in a world that constantly pressures us to conform.

Where does our fear of being different come from? Well, everything you've read so far should have you thinking that some of it is simply the result of living in the U.S. of G. However, all human beings have a primal, biologically based tendency to fear falling out with a group. The best explanation for this phenomenon lies in the fact that early humans needed social organization to survive. Only in groups were people able to defend, feed, shelter and nurture themselves with any efficiency. It makes sense, then, that we developed a drive to bond and a fear of losing contact with others.

Fortunately, in our modern world, survival does not depend on constant conformity to the rules of a social group. In fact, we enjoy the privilege of striking our own balance between independence and attachment, individuality and group involvement. Although all of us must adhere to the laws and contracts that make us safe and bring order to daily life, we can be very creative when it comes to personal relationships, work, home, spirituality and most other elements of life. We live in a time of extraordinary freedom, when most of our limits are determined by our basic practical needs and our own willingness to take risks.

How willing are you to take risks in order to be *Real*? You will discover the answer as you move gradually and deliberately toward your self-designed life. Say you recall that you once loved tennis. The movement, the challenge to improve, the competition—all of it used to make you feel intensely alive. One way to take a small risk and reclaim this part of the *Real* you might be to sign up for some tennis lessons with the idea of getting back in the game.

You will feel anxious, maybe even a little fearful, as you approach that first lesson. You may wonder: *How will I look? What will people think? Maybe I'm too clumsy, too old, too flabby.* But summon just a little bit of courage—that power that helps us act even when we are uncomfortable—and you will learn whether tennis can be part of the *Real* you today.

If you have trouble with even the first small steps toward your *Real* self, remember that you never have to be the best at tennis, or anything else you try. In fact, the very idea that we must excel at what we attempt or risk terrible shame is one of the most destructive myths of the *Object* culture. Too many of us are sidelined by an inordinate fear of failure, as if falling short is somehow disgraceful.

Failure is among the most misunderstood of all common human experiences. As children, when our lives are consumed with the struggles and joys of learning new things every day, we understand that mistakes and missteps are normal. But by the time we reach adulthood, many of us feel a profound aversion to getting anything wrong. Failure, especially a failure that others see, becomes mortifying.

These feelings of shame are reinforced by the *Thinglish* terms that our society attaches to failure. In the *Thinglish* language, people who try but fall short of a goal are regarded as "losers," "screw-ups" and worse. They are considered to be the shamed opposites of the winners in our world. One of the most *Objectifying* versions of this kind of *Thinglish* is the phrase "one of life's losers," which I have heard applied to people who don't fulfill some arbitrary social definition of success. These terms require us to accept someone else's priorities and definitions. They reflect a fearful way of living. When we hear someone use them, they are almost always a reflection of his or her own inhibiting and self-limiting anxieties. When you call someone else a "loser," you are *Really* expressing your own fear of being a "loser" yourself. Once you have accepted that life is not a matter of winning and losing but rather a long journey of development, discovery and experience, terms like *"winner"* and *"loser"* cease to be part of your daily vocabulary. More important, they stop circulating in your mind, producing fear and dread like the background music for a scary movie.

The wonderful thing about letting go of the fear of failure is that it liberates us to try new experiences and new relationships. Once you know in your heart that *Real* inventiveness, creativity and even love are impossible without the lessons we learn from failure, you feel more courageous about making an effort. Consider an obvious example: man's experience with flight. You've seen the composite films showing one experimental airplane after another crashing. Without these crashes, the Wright brothers, who had their own share of failures, would have never succeeded. The same was true for the scientists who developed the polio vaccine (people actually died because of their failures) and the engineers who developed suspension bridges (more than a few fell down). Finally, who among us has been able to find love without first experiencing heartbreak? Relationships that end are not failures. They are simply learning experiences that help us all define what *Real* love is on our own terms. In every breakup we can find clues to our heart's true desires and the courage to try again.

Every *Real* person I have ever known or heard about defines failure as a learning experience, not a defeat. This is true for a professional golfer I know, who "loses" almost every tournament he plays, but doesn't feel like a loser because he lives the life of his dreams. It is true for every successful performer, salesman, artist or businessperson. Failure is built into their lives, yet they keep going because they love the process of what they are doing, not just the result.

A good example of this in my own life comes from my experiments in the world of pottery-making. I took classes, enjoyed my time at the wheel and eagerly awaited the pieces that baked in the kiln. Slowly, I created a collection of what I came to call, in a loving way, "my little uglies." The cups, pitchers and bowls I made were, let's just say, not quite perfect. But I didn't feel like they were failures. I believed they were reflections of my effort to learn about pottery and, more importantly, my own interest in making things. Eventually I moved on to other mediums and found I was a better painter than potter. But I kept a few of those precious uglies as reminders of those happy hours of discovery.

All I needed to transform my uglies from shameful failures into cute little symbols of my *Real* creative self was the proper perspective or, you might say, the right set of beliefs. This was possible because I hadn't set out to create *Objects* of great monetary value. From my very first class I chose to speak to myself in a kind and positive way. I was after long-term growth rather than immediate, short-term achievement. I believed that no matter how my pieces came out, I could feel proud. Failures—misshapen forms, imperfect glazing, uneven colors—were nothing to be ashamed of. I was able to consider my experience in this light because my perspective was a matter of deliberate choices. I decided that:

Failure leads to growth. It is practically a cliché to say that we all learn more from failure than success, but this is true. The greatest achievements almost always involve setbacks, and it is the experience of falling short that leads us to a more successful approach.

New beliefs are powerful. Your positive *beliefs* can

remove the stigma from failure. If you truly believe there is honor and value in trying your best, and risking failure, then you profit even if you don't reach your goal.

Courage comes with experience. I see courage grow in this natural way every time I meet with my students at the college where I teach. The school was founded with the sole purpose of educating adult men and women—most are over age thirty—who don't fit into the cookie-cutter version of higher education. The college offers small group seminars and one-on-one teaching by "mentors" who collaborate with students on custom-made degree programs. While the work is every bit as demanding as it would be at any other college—our graduates have become scientists, business executives, professionals and more—every effort is made to accommodate them as individuals.

Because they are returning to school years and sometimes even decades after they last sat in a classroom, my first-time students are almost always anxious, self-doubting and a little afraid. Some had such negative school experiences in the past that just enrolling shows enormous courage. But with just a little coaching to change their beliefs about themselves and the purpose of education—it's not just about acquiring a degree but about developing yourself—almost everyone begins to thrive. Although the other professors I work with might not say it this way, I believe that the students I teach are all embarking on the journey to *Real.*

One of the great paradoxes of being *Real* is that while we fear it will isolate us, it almost always brings us closer to other people. Indeed, by bravely showing our families, friends and others what we value, aspire to and dream about, we can develop relationships that are based on who we *Really* are, rather than on a false *Object* image that is constructed to satisfy what we think others expect of us. And when we are freed from all the strain of having to present a generic façade, we have the energy to pay closer attention to others.

Of course, some people will have trouble adapting to the emergence of the *Real* you. This is especially true of those who believed they benefited from your willingness to bend to certain limitations. For example, you may start taking more time for yourself, and your spouse may feel left out. Or you may put limits on the overtime you accept at work, making your boss feel like she has lost a valuable resource.

In these situations it helps to use a little diplomacy and a lot of tact. Don't shake this book in your husband's face and declare, "It's time for me to get *Real*, and I won't let you stop me!" Instead, consider making changes in a gradual way. Don't abandon people you love or a job that is essential to paying the bills. When necessary, explain what you are doing in a way that shows that the change you seek shouldn't hurt anyone else. Among the points you might make are:

I'm rediscovering some parts of me that I let go of.

I'm trying new things that make me feel better about myself.

I'm trying to deal with that burned-out feeling that's been bothering me.

I think I can be a better friend/partner/spouse/worker/parent if I can learn to be better to myself.

The process of becoming *Real* can produce a peaceful revolution in your life, not a war. It is likely to make you more attractive, more interesting and more appealing to those who love you, because they have been instinctively drawn to the *Real* parts of you all along. Finally, it is quite likely that the changes others see in you will spark both admiration and curiosity. When people ask about what is happening, you can tell them you have decided to throw off the anxieties and fears that have limited you in the past and begun searching for the life that will make you *Really* you. The result, as in the story of the Velveteen Rabbit, will be more than you ever expected.

And then a strange thing happened. For where a tear had fallen, a flower grew out of the ground. . . . It was so beautiful that the little Rabbit forgot to cry, and just lay there watching it. And presently the blossom opened, and out of it there stepped a fairy.

Velveteen

Principle #6

Real Is Honest

"The mechanical toys were very superior ... and pretended they were real . . . Even Timothy, the jointed wooden lion . . . put on airs and pretended he was connected with Government."

Only one of Margery Williams's characters—the Skin Horse—is honest and *Real* throughout the entire story and doesn't pretend to be something he's not. He is the one whose example piques the little Rabbit's curiosity. And when the Rabbit turns to him with questions, the Skin Horse is kindly, sensitive and, in the end, always truthful. If he weren't, the Rabbit would never learn all he needs to know in order to become *Real* himself.

The honesty of the Skin Horse begins with the way he thinks about himself. He is flawed and a bit scarred, but he is not sensitive about his appearance. Instead, he affirms that although life has left him somewhat tattered in comparison with the newer mechanical toys of the nursery, these imperfections are what make him unique and interesting.

This ability to be clear-eyed about yourself is the most important element of what I call *Real* honesty. Being honest about yourself may seem like a very difficult thing to do. In fact, I think a lot of us actually avoid learning things about ourselves because we are afraid of what we'll discover.

Much of this fear is the irrational by-product of a belief that we must be perfect. Some of it flows from the fact that deep down, we all know that we are made of a complete array of qualities and traits—some very appealing, some not so attractive—simply because we are human. Accepting this, and knowing that perfection is impossible, makes it much easier to drop your old defensiveness and take a closer look at yourself. While you're at it, consider also these truths about perfection:

Perfection is arbitrary. Whether we consider the human body, or a work of art, so-called perfection is based on standards that can be changed. Would the woman who had the perfect figure in 1950 meet today's standards?

Perfection is boring. Certain objects are flawless. But how long will a diamond hold your attention? And what makes one perfect diamond different from another with the same size, cut, color and clarity? Nothing very interesting.

Human perfection is ultimately impossible. You cannot name a hero who wasn't flawed in some way. This is because life is too varied and challenging for anyone to get all of it right.

Many people come to me for therapy saying they are "totally screwed up." This is never true. Once you allow yourself to look inward, rather than focusing on outside distractions, you will be pleasantly surprised.

There's a lot to like in the *Real* you, and being honest means recognizing these positives first. Maybe you are kind, patient, considerate or inquisitive. Maybe you have a talent for teaching, building or nurturing others. The possibilities are endless, and if you will just open yourself up to them, you will undoubtedly recognize a long list of things that will make you proud and happy. I suggest you write them down and keep the list in a place where you can review it during times when you feel unsure about yourself. If you have trouble doing this, try:

The Admiration Inventory

Sit in a quiet place with pen and paper. Draw a line down the middle of a sheet of paper to make two columns.

On the left side, write a list of the names of people you admire. Include anyone you admire for aspects other than their appearance. On the right side, list your reasons for admiring them. Chances are, you'll be writing about their special talents, virtues, strengths and values and the ways in which these have been evident in their life choices.

Once the list is complete, fold the paper along the centerline so that only the list of traits can be read. Take a good, long look. Read them carefully, because the things you admire in others are also a part of you. Some of them may be traits you have quietly tried to develop and live by. Maybe you're feeling ashamed because you don't see those traits evident in the way you're living right now. That's a valuable piece of information. Now you have an informed choice—are you living as a person you admire, or do you have changes you'd like to make? As I often say to my clients, feel it, face it, fix it. The ball is in your court.

You aren't convinced? Then allow yourself to take one more risk. If you have a partner, lover or very close friend, ask him or her what made you attractive back when you first met. Of course, it's a good idea to share your first impressions of them, too. But allow yourself to listen as he or she describes you in those early days of the relationship. Be honest enough with yourself to admit that he or she saw some very *Real* and very good things in you. Those things haven't gone away.

If you don't feel confident bringing others into your process, think back to times when you felt proud of yourself, or times when you felt most ashamed—clues to the *Real* you are hidden in those memories. Maybe you felt most proud when you were the only one in school who could answer a question about an obscure topic that interested you. Maybe the *Real* you needs to return to exploring that topic further, or to situations where your intelligence is honored more fully or more often.

You can excavate more signs of the honest-to-goodness you by sharing memories with old friends or exploring school report cards and yearbooks. Look for anything that will tell you about the interests you pursued through your life, the goals you achieved and the people you loved. They all bear honest evidence of the positive parts of the *Real* you.

You may have been taught to avoid taking credit for the good things you have done and the good qualities you possess. I'm not suggesting that you race around telling everyone how great you are. But I am saying that in order to be *Real* you must accept your gifts and live with them. Be honest enough to drop your defenses and your fear of standing out, and recognize that you are a good and worthy person.

There is another side of being *Really* honest with yourself. (You knew we were going to get to this, didn't you?) Of course I am talking about accepting, even embracing, the parts of ourselves that we would rather not recognize.

I know that the prospect of being honest with yourself about things you'd like to deny is scary. But remember, perfection is one of the *Big Lies* of the *Object* culture. No one is perfect. More importantly, no one is *supposed* to be perfect.

When my children were young, I taught them to let go of perfectionism when we baked chocolate chip cookies. As we followed the recipe, we talked about how store-bought cookies all looked the same—perfectly round, evenly spaced chips, same number of chips per cookie—because they're made by machines. But homemade cookies are made by people who put love and care into each one. A homemade cookie isn't going to be perfectly round, and the number of chips may vary. It might even get burned on the bottom. But eating it is more satisfying, because it connects you to the baker. A homemade cookie is a complete emotional transaction. Its imperfections only add to the experience.

Once you accept that imperfections are what make us each homemade, it becomes much easier to explore those traits you fear are negative. And it is this exploration that reduces and eventually eliminates the shame we attach to our shortcomings. If "perfect" isn't your goal, but *Realness* is, imperfections are less shameful.

I can give you two examples, one serious and one lighthearted, of how honesty freed me from shame in my own life. When I was a teenager I developed a very sarcastic and destructive sense of humor, in part as a way to cover up my own insecurities. Once I started to be more honest about myself, I was able to acknowledge that I sometimes hurt people with my jokes. Getting *Real* allowed me to look at my behavior and make changes.

I'm not saying it was easy. For a while, I felt ashamed and confused about the times I had hurt other people with my words. I also felt uncomfortable around those I had hurt. But if I was going to be *Real*, I had to recognize that my failing was very human and forgivable. Then, when the impulse to be sarcastic was building, I knew I had options—like leaving or taking the time to compose myself so that I could express my feelings in a productive, less abusive manner.

Knowing I could be hard on other people allowed me to adopt one other effective strategy: apologizing. Whenever I hurt someone, I immediately admitted it and said I was sorry. Remarkably, this act always brought me closer to the person I may have hurt. This will happen when you are honest about your own failings. This is because sincere apologies are almost always followed by forgiveness and closeness.

It's paradoxical, but true. Being wrong and being *Real* about it can make us feel closer to others and better about ourselves. I actually feel hopeful every time I discover that something I did caused a problem with another person. I feel optimistic because I know that I can address the issue, and in taking responsibility I can feel happier about who I am.

Now, I also promised a less serious example of my imperfect self. There are many to choose from, but one has become the source of much laughter in my family. I am a worrier. I worry about car crashes, plane crashes, fires, carbon monoxide poisoning—you name it. And sometimes my worrying, however well intentioned, is annoying.

For a long time I insisted that my safety concerns were entirely reasonable and that other people, especially my children and my husband, should take them all seriously.

Fortunately, when I developed the honesty to face this odd little fixation, I realized that I sometimes take it to the extreme. Once I was able to claim my safety anxiety and explain to my family that I knew it was "just one of those weird Toni things," they felt less irritated by it. They became more patient with my concerns and even coined a nickname for me—FEMA—the acronym for the Federal Emergency Management Agency. They call me that nickname when I'm overdoing it, like when I worry about a big ferry boat capsizing on a calm, cloud-less day.

My experience as FEMA, the beloved worrier, shows that when you are *Real* and can accept, even embrace, your own peculiarities, other people will too. Where once my husband and daughters thought I was a safety nag, they now understand that my anxiety is a sign of my love for them. This often happens when we express the honest truth about ourselves. Aren't you always more inclined to move closer to someone when you understand what they're about?

Once we learn how to be honest and accepting when it comes to ourselves, we can be more honest in our responses to others. This doesn't mean just passing judgment or being critical. It means adopting a *Realistic* view of human nature that allows you to accept the mistakes people make, and even forgive and forget everyday outrages and annoyances.

Margery Williams gave the Skin Horse, who is the happiest and wisest citizen of the nursery, all these qualities. He knew he was threadbare and shabby and that his tail had been loved to the point where it was a scraggly mess. But he also saw others with a clear and honest eye and recognized that even those who seemed unblemished would one day break down. There was nothing to be gained from hiding or denying that fact. And honestly embracing it made it possible for him to be truly happy and at peace.

He was wise, for he had seen a long succession of mechanical toys arrive to boast and swagger and by-and-by break their main-springs and pass away, and he knew that they were only toys, and would never turn into anything else.

Velveteen

Principle #7

Real Is Generous

And then one day the Boy was ill. His face grew flushed and he talked in his sleep, and his little body was so hot that it burned the Rabbit when he held him close. Strange people came and went in the nursery, and a light burned all night and through it all the little Velveteen Rabbit lay there, hidden from sight under the bedclothes, and he never stirred, for he was afraid that if they found him someone might take him away, and he knew that the Boy needed him.

Because the transformation is gradual, the Velveteen Rabbit shows the signs of being *Real* long before he notices it himself or anyone declares that he has crossed some threshold. It's evident for every reader to see during the Boy's terrible illness, which is the biggest crisis in the book. Even though he is being burned, the Rabbit is concerned only about the Boy. He gives generously of himself, despite the discomfort, because his finely tuned sense of empathy tells him that he has an important role to play.

This kind of generosity does not involve handing over boxes tied with ribbons. Instead, it is an expression of a certain spirit of goodwill and encouragement. When we are generous in this way, we support people when they need us most, not when it is most convenient for us. And we support them as they strive to become authentic and *Real* themselves.

This can be done in two ways. First, we can get behind the people we know and love whenever they pursue a goal or express their hopes and dreams. I'm not talking about supportive words alone. If someone tells you she wants to go to college, but is confused about how to get there, you can share what you know about higher education, and even go to the library with her to gather information. This is *Real* generosity that involves giving of yourself.

The second kind of generosity—the spirit that moves us to freely encourage the aspirations of others—is a bit more general. It calls for us to change the world we inhabit in whatever ways we can to make it more humane and tolerant of people with different needs and abilities.

Generosity is in short supply because so many of us fear that the world is not able to supply everyone's needs. This fear, matched with insecurity, leads us to accept one of the *Object* culture's basic tenets: that competition is the essence of modern life. In fact, the value of competition is so widely accepted that we all know the slogans used to promote it:

Competition brings out the best. According to this widely accepted notion, a fierce contest is the only way to identify worthy creations, performances and people. Those who believe in this concept apply it to everything: education, art, dating, business and religion. In the end, if you follow this ideal, you reach another of the universal beliefs of the *Object* culture, which says . . .

Someone must always win and someone must always lose. If you believe this, then you go into every encounter with other people worrying about what you might lose and scheming to gain some sort of advantage. You take this approach because you accept the validity of a third erroneous assumption—that the rewards available in this world are in limited supply and therefore . . .

Winning is everything. In the world of *Objects,* the only way that you can establish your value and gain the admiration or support of others is through winning. This means that your value as a person can be measured in dollars and cents, horsepower, square footage or even the numbers on the bathroom scale.

Altogether, these axioms describe a society in which we must always strive against each other for the basic necessities of life. There is no room in this dynamic for generosity. Indeed, acts of kindness toward would-be competitors are deemed foolish.

Unfortunately, much of what we experience reinforces this view. Our jobs are less secure than they once were. Half of all marriages end in divorce. And we tend to move from one community to another much more often than previous generations. Given all this isolation and uncertainty, it's no wonder so many of us adopt a fearful, me-against-the-world stance. From this position, it's impossible to be generous.

But the *Real* truth that is ignored by all those who would make competition the basis of modern life is that there is enough—enough love, enough wealth, enough comfort and care—for every living person on this planet. And we don't have to be afraid to be generous, because when we give to others, it simply increases the overall supply of what is good and positive in the world.

People have understood the magic of generosity for as long as we have lived as social beings. This is because the earliest societies were based on a form of generosity called reciprocity.

In its most basic and primitive form, reciprocity is a simple exchange. I help you catch an antelope for dinner. You help me cook it. In modern terms, I may help shovel your driveway when it snows. You help me with mine after the next storm. Human beings have used this kind of trading ever since they began living in groups.

The higher level of reciprocity that occurs when you are *Really* generous does not depend on immediate repayment of favors. In fact, it is practiced without any conscious thought of a future reward. We give because we can, because it feels good, and because it fosters a more trusting, generous society in which everyone gives according to his or her abilities.

Reciprocity works in every setting. At your job, for example, you may be enlisted to train a new employee. Chances are you won't receive extra pay, and the boss will expect you to keep performing your own duties. If you approach this task with sullen resentment, there's a good chance that you will damage your own standing in the company. But if you are open and generous there's a very good chance that you will create an ally who will be on your side for years. That new employee might rise to be your boss and offer you more help than you could have extended when you shepherded her through those first weeks on the job.

Before we move our focus away from generosity in the workplace, I'd like to make one last and perhaps surprising point. Generosity is good for the bottom line. Although some business gurus still champion greed and self-interest, most experts now say that teamwork, mentoring and a so-called win-win approach work better in the long run. Among coworkers, these values are conducive to the kind of creativity, productivity and communication that keeps a company sharp. When it comes to the marketplace, generosity drives firms to offer high quality and fair value, which is what most customers are looking for.

If you practice it enough, generosity become a habit. One of my clients offered a wonderful example of how *Real* people act in generous ways as a matter of course. Despite a divorce and rather bad luck when it came to making money, Helen raised her three children with great warmth and attention and sacrificed to give them a comfortable life and good education.

But in my eyes, the most generous thing Helen did involved her devotion to animals. In the time I have known her, she has adopted a blind dog, rescued numerous old, injured tortoises and taken in many abandoned cats. These rescues have saved her local shelter from the expense of caring for these animals. But Helen would never consider the time and money she devotes to them a sacrifice, because these acts help her to feel good about herself and bring great warmth to her everyday life.

Because she is smart and sensible, Helen limits her animal rescues and will never become one of those people who take in more animals than they can handle, only to end up neglecting them all. She understands that there is such a thing as too much giving. When it comes to human beings, it can be harder to draw the line. But I would argue that we must always stop before generosity limits our ability to help ourselves.

This is the classic fish-versus-fisherman concept. Indeed, it is always better to help someone learn to fish than to give him a fish. We can avoid the mistake of hurting others with our help if we understand that a truly generous act always helps someone become stronger, more capable and better able to help themselves. The idea is not to make over someone in our own image, but to promote their development as individuals. This means having enough empathy to find out what someone needs and when they need it.

It feels wonderful to help someone in the way they want to be helped. One of the most gratifying moments in my private practice occurred when a woman told me at the end of her treatment, "You gave me ME. Now I don't have to pretend to be happy when I'm not. I've learned that I can just tell people that I'm not happy today. If they want to accept me when I'm moody and cranky, okay; if not, let's get together another time. And they know that I accept them, too."

My client demonstrates how generosity multiplies and grows. For this reason, it is the ultimate expression of our *Real* inner selves, our spirits or, if you prefer, our souls. It is one sure way to counter the values of the *Object* culture, create *Real* relationships and touch more people than you'll ever know.

Velveteen

Principle #8

Real Is Grateful

"You must have your old bunny," [Nana] said. "Fancy all that fuss for a toy!" The Boy sat up in his bed and stretched out his hands. "Give me my Bunny!" he said. "You mustn't say that. He isn't a toy. He's real!" When the little Rabbit heard that, he was happy, for he knew that what the Skin Horse had said was true at last. The nursery magic had happened to him. And he was a toy no longer. He was Real. The Boy himself had said it.

It is easy to tell that the happiness felt by the Velveteen Rabbit as the Boy corrected his Nana— "You mustn't say that"—is infused with another deep feeling that made the experience even more wonderful—gratitude. After all, the Rabbit knows that the Boy's love has played a big role in his transformation. And the little Bunny understands that he should be grateful for a bold affirmation—"He's real!"—from such an important friend. Acts of kindness, after all, aren't a right we possess, but a gift we are given.

Of course, the Rabbit would not have felt all that gratitude and happiness if he had been distracted. The key to his experience was the fact that he was focused and fully present. This kind of attentiveness almost always reveals to us little moments of grace that can make our hearts swell with gratitude, too.

Take for example the counseling session I had with an anxious young man named Kevin, who once brought his camera to our meeting. He said he was worried about his next assignment in a photography class, which called for him to shoot pictures that emphasized light and dark, shapes and shadows.

It was late afternoon and the setting sun was shining brightly into my office. As we spoke about some other issue—perhaps it was schoolwork, his parents or his friends—I noticed that he kept glancing to his right. I finally turned to see what was catching his eye.

The sunlight was casting beautiful shadows of a tropical plant onto the wall. I told Kevin he could take out his camera and snap a photo if he wanted to.

"I *was* listening to you," he said, nervously. "I heard everything you said."

"I know, but if you want the picture you can take it."

"Okay, just this one picture, and then I'm done."

He took the picture. But every ten minutes, as the light shifted and the shadow changed, we agreed that he could take another photo. Our talk went well. And we both enjoyed the simple gift of sunlight and shadow.

If I were asked to sum up how we felt when the hour was over, I would say that we were both grateful to have been in the same time and place together. He learned that it's okay to slow down and notice what's in your environment. I was grateful that I had the opportunity to show him that adults don't have to exert rigid control in every setting.

Kevin and I had shared our appreciation—and gratitude—for something simple and beautiful. We were able to feel grateful because we had allowed ourselves to be empathetic, honest and patient—in short, *Real*.

Gratitude flows when you are able to focus on the positive instead of the negative. The Velveteen Rabbit does this when he adapts to being the Boy's bedtime companion and realizes the value in their close relationship.

In contrast, the Boy's Nana is unable to see what's going on in the nursery and voices plenty of impatience and negativity. Those two emotions are sure signs of a person who is not yet *Real* enough to be grateful for the simple gifts of life—relationships, nature, the passing of time.

> "Here," she said, "take your old Bunny! He'll do to sleep with you!" And she dragged the Rabbit out by one ear, and put him into the Boy's arms.

No doubt Nana never learned to recognize and be grateful for the beauty all around her, including beautiful relationships like the one between the Boy and the Rabbit. Unfortunately, many of us haven't learned this kind of gratitude either. This is because many (if not most) children first learn about gratitude when their parents instruct them to say, "Thank you." Often this is done in the context of teaching good manners. You are served ice cream for dessert. You say, "Thank you."

Trouble arises when the lessons become layered with pressure, and worse, guilt. A little boy gets a present and the first thing his mother says is, "What do you say?" Suddenly a positive experience becomes a pop quiz. Worse, if the child doesn't feel genuine gratitude (maybe the present was a three-pack of underwear) he's forced to tell a white lie by saying, "Thank you," when he really wants to say, "This is a present?"

If you grew up in a home where your mother or father felt free to communicate disappointment and resentment, they likely added big portions of shame and guilt to their demands for gratitude. *Thinglish* questions like, "This is the thanks I get?" and "I've given you every *thing*. Why aren't you happy?" turn gratitude into an *Object* that can be demanded at any moment.

Dissatisfaction with things is one of the engines that drive our economy. Commercial messages aim to make us feel unhappy with the things we own, and worse, who we are, so that we will spend money to feel better. This never works because every season brings a new and improved menu of things to buy, and what you have, or who you are, is declared obsolete and inadequate. No wonder so many of us have trouble feeling good about much of anything. We are uncomfortable with gifts, favors or even kind words because we fear there are strings attached. And we have trouble feeling gratitude for the blessings of life because we're always focused on what we don't possess.

Fortunately, gratitude involves much more than feeling good about something you own or saying, "Thank you," for someone's kind act. True gratitude involves understanding there is something beautiful and marvelous in almost everything around you.

This is especially true when you notice the many ways that people grow and develop and express themselves. With the right eye you can see that the talents, quirks, creations and achievements of the people you encounter are incredible illustrations of the variety and tenacity of the human spirit.

I can offer a good example for parents. Perhaps you are raising a little boy who has extraordinary amounts of energy and a certain "I'll do it my way" temperament. Yes, keeping him safe and channeling his energies into something productive will demand more of you. But aren't his challenging qualities the very traits that will make him a success later in life? Isn't it possible to be grateful for the little dynamo he seems to be?

To get to the point where you can feel this type of *Real* gratitude, even in stressful situations, begin by associating gratitude with both *awareness* and *appreciation*. These two skills lead to the kind of heartwarming gratitude that is both genuine and fulfilling.

Awareness. When our minds are receptive and our senses are well-tuned, we become aware of the world around us. I'm sure that you have experienced this. Maybe you gave yourself the gift of a few minutes in a backyard hammock and discovered the symphony made by songbirds. Or perhaps you let yourself get lost in a truly great film and realized that you were able to see every move the actors made and heard all the different messages hidden in the dialogue. People who have become so *Real* that they no longer worry about their self-worth and calmly observe everything in their environment experience this kind of awareness.

Appreciation. When you recognize the value in people, experiences and even certain things, awareness grows into appreciation. You must have experienced this while looking at a great piece of art. You cannot examine a beautiful sculpture or painting without being aware of the talents and time invested by the artist. Once you have this awareness, you appreciate the work's beauty even more.

But are you sensitive enough to bring that aware attitude to more ordinary experiences? Can you appreciate, for example, the effort so many people put into doing their jobs well? Consider something as ordinary as the work done by the carrier who gets the newspaper to your house by seven o'clock every morning. When you walk out to get it, can you imagine him rising early, picking up his bundles of newspapers and driving the route through all kinds of weather? Every morning it's there, without fail, and once you are aware and appreciate it, this tiny event can make you feel grateful.

In the *Object* culture we expect people to talk about the things they long to acquire and to obsess over the troubles in their lives. When we answer the question, "How was your day?" we often automatically describe what went wrong. This frame of mind is a habit for many people, but gratitude can become a habit, too. If it doesn't come naturally, don't worry; with a little conscious effort it's easy to develop it.

Start by reminding yourself to notice the pleasant things you take for granted as you go through the day. Is your home warm and comfortable when the winter winds blow? Did your car start this morning? Was the coffee you bought on the way to work delicious?

This process can work after the fact, too. On many nights, I'll take a few minutes to run through my day and notice the little positive moments that escaped my attention. This is the opposite of a habit many people practice. It's the "you won't believe what happened to me today" habit. You might feel a little relief as you tell your troubles to someone. But I guarantee you that your spirits will go higher if you also appreciate the positive things that occurred.

We can do this, even when we are alone. I make a deliberate effort to write about positive experiences in my journal, especially when I'm feeling stressed or challenged. When I look back at the entries, I notice that most are appreciations of little things: the snuffling purr of an old cat, my daughter's sense of humor, the warmth of my husband's hand on mine.

The practice of gratitude becomes more valuable during very difficult times because it fosters optimism and serves as an antidote to worry. It's hard to be anxious, after all, when you are reflecting on your blessings. It can even work in situations that seem, at first, to offer us nothing but unhappiness. Consider the woman who discovers her partner has been unfaithful. This is a terrible thing to learn, and she will be heartbroken. But nothing is more valuable in a relationship than the truth. And if the truth allows her to get out of a bad situation, or moves the couple to grow and change, then it is something she can eventually feel grateful about.

Ultimately, when you are *Real*, it's even possible to feel gratitude for the progress that effort and fate have allowed you to make toward a self-designed life. This kind of gratitude means you can move forward knowing you didn't waste your time here on Earth bound to someone else's notions of what is good and valuable and important. You will be able to live without regrets.

Velveteen

Principle #9

Real Can Be Painful

"What is real?" asked the Rabbit one day, when they were lying side by side near the nursery fender before Nana came in to tidy the room. "Does it mean having things that buzz inside you and a stick-out handle?" "Real isn't how you are made," said the Skin Horse. "It's something that happens to you. . . . " "Does it hurt?" asked the Rabbit. "Sometimes," said the Skin Horse, for he was always truthful. "When you are Real, you don't mind being hurt."

Margery Williams's little Rabbit had to learn that his transformation from a toy into something *Real* would be a complex process. He wanted the rich, full life that being *Real* promised. But he also had to learn that the awakening was sometimes painful. This is not something you have to seek out. Life brings all of us a measure of pain.

"[Pain is] something that happens to you," as the Skin Horse says.

In fact, the more access you have to your own *Real* thoughts and feelings, the more you will see your own imperfections and limitations. You also hear more clearly the fleeting negative thoughts that are so commonplace we almost don't notice them. These revelations can be quite painful.

When I started to become more *Real*, I began to notice that my mind often wandered to the kind of self-critical phrases that buzz inside many women:

I should diet.

The kitchen's a mess.

How many calories did I consume today? I'm such a pig.

Does my husband still love me?

My hair is a mess.

Who do I think I am?

The neighbors look so much happier.

I'm so ugly/old/flabby.

I'm a mess.

What's wrong with me?

As troubling as they may be, these thoughts and

feelings have great value because they are a remarkably accurate list of the obstacles that lie between you and a *Real* life.

Where do they come from? Some come from the social environment we navigate every day. They are the discontents that are endemic to life in the United States of Generica. Others can be traced to your own experiences with people who encouraged you to discount your true self. Typically, these negative thoughts are planted in our minds by those who believe they are training us to survive in a cold, cruel world.

In my childhood, I was trained to make myself as invisible and self-sufficient as possible. My parents pushed this role on me for a number of reasons. The main one may have been because they were both diagnosed with serious and ultimately debilitating illnesses. They were too distraught to focus on a little girl, and they lacked the physical and emotional energy to take care of me. For these reasons and more, I was discouraged from ever voicing a need or desire. I even learned to hate those parts of myself that required care and attention. I believed I had to be perfect in order to be good enough. As I grew up, I continued to believe I must be perfect, always nurturing and available. Of course, these beliefs set me up for an unhappy life as a resent-ful, empty-hearted martyr.

Once I began to explore my long-dormant emotions, I came to the painful realization that I had been pro-grammed to impose some pretty severe limits on myself. The feelings that this new knowledge evoked were quite powerful. I was angry and resentful, and I grieved over the losses I had experienced. I had spent many years denying myself comfort and even love because deep down inside I believed that a good person didn't seek these things for herself. She only gave them.

As you reflect on your own beliefs and feelings, you will, no doubt, uncover your own emotional traps, set inside your heart without you even knowing it. Every one of my clients has had this experience. One man, I'll call him Tom, was raised by parents whose choices in life had followed very traditional assumptions. His mother stayed at home with the children. His father was a construction worker. They both told him their choices were the best ones anyone could make, and that people who were different were wrongheaded.

Tom received the message loud and clear. Don't insult your parents or siblings by becoming different. The rules in his family declared that "we stick together like birds of a feather—and no one leaves, because it's a betrayal to abandon the family."

Programmed to limit himself, Tom behaved like a bird with clipped wings. Instead of pursuing his dream of a college education, he became a police officer. He settled in a home near his parents, married young and started his own family. He did the right things, according to what he had been taught. It wasn't until his forties that he came to understand how much of himself he had lost. He began to express his *Real* self in the quietest ways. While on late-night watches, he wrote poetry on scraps of paper. At the end of his shift, he stashed his poems in his locker at work. He never even let his wife know they were there. His writings revealed his sensitive nature. His poems were about the nature of life, truth, love and his confusion about who he was.

Although he steadily expanded his own sense of self, Tom did not throw out everything he had been. He continued to work for the police and remained a steadfast man of confidence on whom everyone could rely. But he also allowed himself to explore his own creative abilities and experience a range of emotions. Excited and a bit confused by what he is feeling, Tom is looking forward to the day when he will retire from the force. He hopes that when he does, he will find a way to let his poetic side bloom. He might start by letting his wife, who knows nothing about this side of Tom, read some of his poems.

As he explores and reveals the long-hidden elements of himself, Tom will inevitably feel some grief and anger. This pain is related to lost opportunities and lost aspects of yourself, which you were pushed to reject. "Wouldn't I have been happier if I had given my creative side some freedom?" you might ask. "Who would I be now if I had been permitted to take my own hopes more seriously?" The anger comes with the knowledge that you were taught to feel ashamed of feelings, desires and dreams that, on their own, are not shameful at all.

For most people, especially those who have not buried serious trauma or abuse in their past, the intense feelings associated with lost pieces of their *Real* selves will pass. But in a small percentage of people, opening up emotionally can produce an especially powerful flood of emotion. If you experience intense feelings that prevent you from functioning in your life, disrupt important relationships and produce the debilitating symptoms of depression—a persistent "down" feeling, loss of appetite, inability to sleep or the need for excessive amounts of sleep—it is a good idea to consult a mental health professional. For some of us, depression or post-traumatic stress disorder is part of our *Reality*. These conditions do not prevent us from becoming our *Real* selves, and they should not be ignored. As we will see later, *Real* can be quite resilient.

The pain of awakening will pass, but that doesn't mean you automatically enter a permanent state of bliss. Instead, if we choose to become more sensitive to our own feelings and thoughts, and the experience of others, we must expect to feel more pain—not less—as we move through our lives.

Why does this happen? First of all, a *Real* person who abandons the generic, numbed-out viewpoint of the *Object* national majority is going to see the negative aspects of our culture more clearly. You will see how people are harmed by rigid stereotypes and feel their pain a little more keenly. You may also experience a greater sense of disappointment as the everyday cruelties you witness come into sharper focus. When a boss puts down your coworker or a parent slaps a child in the mall, it will bother you.

Your more sensitive and *Realistic* perspective may also change how you feel when you are with old friends and relatives. A visit with family may remind you of incidents or attitudes that robbed you of your individuality or sense of self-worth. Long-time friends and acquaintances may suddenly seem more shallow and less supportive. You may find yourself wondering, "How could I have spent all that time talking with her about shopping?" Or you might encounter hostility because you "seem different" to people who have known you for years.

Fortunately, we don't have to explain ourselves to every critic or dwell in regret over "what might have been." If you realize that you have been affected by negative messages, you can start to replace those old painful thoughts with your own ideas about what makes you a worthy person and what makes life good. This is, for many people, a frightening concept. Few of us have much experience with making free choices that respect our own values and not the messages we get from friends, family and society. The prospect of deciding among what can seem like endless options can be intimidating, even paralyzing. To make this easier, remember that there are probably many parts of your current life that fit you perfectly for now. Being *Real* doesn't mean changing everything for the sake of change. Think about this journey as a flower slowly opening, rather than fireworks exploding. It's a slow process of self-discovery.

And remember, all true interests and desires have value and deserve respect. Not everyone has an inner artist or poet. One of my clients, a woman named Kate, discovered she loves to crunch numbers. As she became *Real*, it became obvious that working alone, balancing accounts in an office building where others are available for support when needed, made her happiest. She had tried working in a bank but learned that she didn't appreciate being interrupted by customers. She wanted to be left to her own devices. Now she does accounts receivable for a large corporation and very much enjoys her work. She has told me that she doesn't understand how I do what I do for my work. She would find it stressful and unpredictable, since the answers aren't clear-cut. I would be miserable doing her job, and she would be miserable doing mine. These differences are what make *Real* people so fascinating.

Don't let the world tell you that your true desires aren't worth pursuing. Instead, take a moment to remember the times you were happy, exhilarated, peaceful or confident. Spend time exploring those memories in detail, possibly even writing down what you recall. The act of writing, even if it's for a readership of one (yourself), will stimulate your memory and help you see yourself more clearly. If you find yourself blocked, consider the following childhood photograph exercise:

Find a photograph from your childhood and place it on a desk or table where you have your paper and pen. Take time to just look at the photo. Think about the child you were at the age the picture was taken; consider who she was with all the compassion you can muster.

Think of her in the same way you would think about your own child, or a favorite niece or nephew. Think about her basic human beauty, potential, dreams and interests.

Now, write a simple physical description of the child in the photo. What color are her eyes, her hair, her clothes? Does she appear confident? Is she feeling silly? Serious? You decide.

Once that physical description is complete, try writing about what the child was like *on the inside* when the photo was taken. Let her talk. Let her tell you what she thought about being photographed, and more importantly, let her tell you who she intends to be when she grows up.

After this exercise, you will find it easier to visit other moments of your life and write about them. The discoveries you will make about the passions, interests, dreams and talents you had *before* the *Object* culture did its damage will be clues to what can be *Real* in adult life.

I saw this happen with Joseph, who came to me convinced he had never been happy in his entire life except for when he was the star pitcher on his high-school baseball team. He had injured his knee, so he was sure that he couldn't play ball anymore and therefore could never be happy again. We began by listing what he enjoyed about being a baseball pitcher. His list included things like:

• A feeling of control over the game. As he accepted or rejected signals from the catcher, his decisions were trusted.

- He loved exercising outdoors.
- The admiration he received.
- His shyness wasn't a problem, because interpersonal skills weren't necessary.
- He felt mysterious rather than conspicuous.

The outcome of this discussion was quite remarkable. Joseph began to see that if he could recapture some of the positive elements of his experience as a teenage ballplayer in his current life, he might reexperience some of those lost feelings.

The realization that he could enjoy the same feelings he knew as a pitcher sparked a new passion for life in Joseph. As he continues his process of becoming *Real*, he can look for relationships, work and other experiences that bring him those feelings of competence, accomplishment and recognition. He also has the opportunity to address some of the areas in which he felt weakest as a teen, like his shyness. The fact that Joseph discovered some qualities he wanted to change, as well as some he will use to create his new self, should not be surprising. We should all expect a similar experience.

The process of becoming *Real* involves acknowledging pain and loss, but it also includes recovering valuable pieces of ourselves and dealing with beliefs and feelings that cause us harm. Each of us is like a crazy quilt of talents, values and dreams, sewn together into a unified whole. And each quilt is different, fascinating and precious.

Velveteen Principle #10

Real Is Flexible

. . . [H]e saw two strange beings creep out of the tall bracken near him. They were rabbits like himself, but quite furry and brand new. They must have been very well made, for their seams didn't show at all, and they changed shape in a queer way when they moved; one minute they were long and thin and the next minute fat and bunchy, instead of staying the same, like he did.

Toward the end of Margery Williams's story, the Velveteen Rabbit sees, for the first time, *Real* rabbits at play in the garden. He notices their beauty—fine fur, no seams—but is most intrigued by how they move. Their bodies flex and bend, seeming to change shape in dramatic ways. The Velveteen Rabbit looks in vain for their windup mechanisms and marvels as they jump and dance.

Though she focuses on the physical differences between the *Real* bunnies and the not-yet-*Real* Velveteen Rabbit, the point Williams makes for her readers is much broader. The *Real* rabbits are special because they can move and change shape to express themselves and enjoy their existence. In short, they are flexible, and this gives them enormous happiness and pleasure. For us, the example of the live rabbits in the garden suggests an essential requirement for being *Real* ourselves—the ability to adapt to changing circumstances.

Flexibility has always been a vital skill for leaders and pioneers. Historically, great things have been accomplished by people who adapt to changing circumstances and learn from their mistakes. Heroes are those who find creative new responses to threats and obstacles.

In our time, flexibility is no longer reserved for pioneers, heroes and rulers. It is a requirement for anyone who wants to feel safe, happy and fulfilled. This is because we live in an era of enormous change and endless choice. A hundred years ago, the typical man or woman lived and died within fifteen miles of the place he or she was born. He or she worked at a single occupation and was married just once. Today, it is not unusual to change jobs, spouses and homes every few years.

In an environment that is so turbulent, *Object* people can fall apart. In *The Velveteen Rabbit* Margery Williams puts it this way:

> . . . [M]echanical toys arrive to boast and swagger, and by-and-by break their main-springs and pass away.

Inflexible people break down like mechanical toys because they are unable to respond to serious challenges in creative ways. Instead they become so frightened they deny the change that's occurring and reach for something that will help them hide from whatever problem they must resolve. Or they fight tooth and nail to hold on to what they have, even when it's clear that the old ways and the old things are no longer working.

To be happy, we must be able to adapt to change. This is true even when it comes to something as universal as aging. The cult of youth is so powerful that many people feel depressed and even desperate as they reach middle age. The message is loud and clear: if you aren't young and beautiful, you are invisible. So instead of accepting, adjusting and embracing the benefits of those years of experience, we fight to stay young and feel devastated when we can no longer run as fast, work as hard or turn as many heads as we used to.

Refusing to adapt can be dangerous. I saw this in stark terms in my brief work with Howard, a man of fifty. Howard was being targeted for layoff from a very stressful, demanding job. In truth, the job better suited workers half his age. But Howard was determined to keep up with, and even surpass, the others. He turned to cocaine for false bursts of energy and confidence. In the short term, the drug gave him what he wanted. But over time he became confused and exhausted.

In our first session, Howard talked about his job as if it were life itself, and he said that if he were fired "it would kill me." With just a little bit of digging, we were able to discover that he felt he would be a worthless failure without the money and status he received from his work. Howard also admitted that by focusing on his job, he had been able to deny the loneliness and grief that struck him after he was divorced from his wife.

Howard began to reconsider what a job loss might mean. He started to think about other work he might enjoy and adjustments he might make in his lifestyle— a smaller house, an older car—that would allow him to get by on a smaller paycheck. He started to feel excited about redefining himself as something more than a job.

Sadly, his cocaine use exacerbated a latent heart condition, and he died before the layoff notice arrived.

Extreme as this example may be, it does help us see that learning to be flexible is not a choice, but a requirement, if we are ever to be *Really* happy and fulfilled. This can be done by adjusting your beliefs about change and how it affects your life:

- **Change does not equal disaster.** I'm not saying it doesn't hurt. Changes like a divorce or getting fired are painful, but change in and of itself won't kill you. Your response to change, on the other hand, can be destructive—or constructive.
- **Change is natural.** Without it, we never experience growth, and without growth, we wither. The *Real* perspective embraces change.
- **Change does not mean you failed.** Change occurs when an old situation no longer fits you. It's not a signal of failure, but rather a spur to improvement.
- **After a big change, you won't be your old self.** This is true, and it's a good thing. Each new experience adds to the complex tapestry of your *Real* self, with a richer, deeper understanding of life's passages.

These *Realistic* attitudes about change will prepare you to be flexible when you have to adjust to new circumstances. A wonderful example of how this can work—and a perfect antidote to the previous story—once rolled into a seminar I was conducting on interpersonal communication.

A former Hell's Angel and alcoholic, Allen had been partially paralyzed in a motorcycle accident. Once he finished grieving and began to adapt, he got sober, then took a job as an advocate with a group that serves the disabled. He devoted himself to wheelchair sports and became an accomplished athlete and competitor.

By the time we met, Allen had used his accident as a catalyst to remake himself in amazing ways. He had more friends, more support and more *Real* love in his life than most people. He was in the middle of planning his wedding. He talked often of other young men in similar situations whose inflexibility led to lives of bitterness and inertia. Their emotional paralysis was far more devastating than their physical disability.

Allen saw the change caused by his accident as both a tragedy and a gift. The tragedy was evident in his paralysis. The gift was obvious, too. It could be seen in the large, expansive life he had built. His ability to adapt to his life-changing accident was aided by his decision to see his accident, in part, as a gift. In doing this he instinctively performed an exercise I call "reframing."

When we reframe a situation, we adopt a new thinking "framework" that gives us a better perspective. Some people use the actual image of a beautiful, gold picture frame to remind themselves of this handy tool. After all, you can make even the ugliest picture look a lot better with the right frame. The same thing happens when we "reframe" the troubling events in our lives in order to find the opportunities that hide there.

For a sense of how well this can work out, consider the moment in *The Velveteen Rabbit* when the Boy moves his bunny into his bed. The Rabbit is very uncomfortable at first, "for the Boy hugged him very tight, and sometimes he rolled over on him, and sometimes he pushed him so far under the pillow that the Rabbit could scarcely breathe." But the Rabbit is flexible enough to adjust. He comes to appreciate the Boy's attention and love. And of course, this love is what sets him firmly on the path to becoming *Real*.

Velveteen
Principle #11

Real Love Endures

Weeks passed, and the little Rabbit grew very old and shabby, but the Boy loved him just as much. He loved him so hard that he loved all his whiskers off, and the pink lining to his ears turned grey, and his brown spots faded. He even began to lose his shape, and he scarcely looked like a rabbit any more, except to the Boy. To him he was always beautiful, and that was all the little Rabbit cared about.

In her story, the devotion and affection that the Boy showers on Margery Williams's Velveteen Rabbit will turn him into a *Real* bunny who comes to accept himself as worthy and lovable no matter what anyone else may say. The message that love helps us grow is obvious.

But well before this transformation is complete, Williams shows us the other ways that *Real* love works.

Besides encouraging the Rabbit's development as a unique individual, the Boy's pure-hearted affection brings the Rabbit happiness, a feeling of self-worth and the ability to offer love in return. The affection he showed was consistent and sincere. And the Boy never asked the Rabbit to be something he was not.

The Boy's relationship with the Velveteen Rabbit points out universal truths about the way love can work in our own lives. As we explore this subject, we'll focus primarily on intimate adult relationships. After all, this is the kind of love we yearn for most once we've passed through adolescence. But keep in mind that most of the basic truths about *Real* love are universal to human relationships.

The generic form of love promoted to devastating effect in the movies and on TV shows favors those who are young and conventionally beautiful. They get to have all the passion, the romance, orgasms like fireworks and first-class airline tickets to Paris on Valentine's Day. Those of us who are less than perfect in appearance hardly ever see anyone who seems remotely like us engaged in on-screen romance or sex. Eventually the experience of watching romance in the movies or on TV leaves us feeling inadequate, unattractive and unlovable.

To overcome these feelings we must remind ourselves that television and film present fantasies—brief scenarios where love conquers all in a few minutes' time—not reality. Nobody in *Real* life enjoys movie-style romance and sex on a day-to-day basis. And if you try to create love based on those false images you are destined to fail.

You don't have to read celebrity magazines to see the futility of love based on *Object* ideals. We all know people who have tried it. My client Karen, for example, was a Wall Street whiz who married a man so handsome you might mistake him for a model. In a short time, however, Karen started having panic attacks, and her husband began rejecting her because he began to see her imperfections. The marriage ended quickly, and Karen decided that, "I'm going to demand a *Real* person next time."

When Karen went back to the dating world she was very brave and very honest. She told men that she wanted more than a superficial relationship, and she warned them that among her imperfections was "this little problem with panic attacks." In order to deal with those attacks she left her high-status job for one she enjoyed more. Then, when she least expected it, a wonderful man came into her life. He loved her as she was. They married, had a baby girl, and are among the least *Objectified* and most loving couples I have ever known.

When you are bravely honest about who you are, potential partners can pick you out in a crowd. They will recognize you as that one-of-a-kind person they have always hoped to find. This has much less to do with how you look than *who you are*. *Real* love flows from shared values, ideals and principles. Remember, the most important and most lovable parts of you are invisible.

And when two *Real* people discover each other, there is absolutely nothing generic about their relationship. They don't try to create cliché romantic situations with rose petals and champagne. Instead they find romantic elements in even the most ordinary circumstances, like grocery shopping or doing the laundry. In fact, when we

Really love someone, we are often struck with an intense emotional reaction when we see them engaged in something that reflects who they are as distinct individuals. If your husband loves fishing and you notice him carefully tying a new fly to use on his next trip to a favorite river, you just love the look of happy focus in his eyes. If your wife is deeply moved by the cycle of life in her garden, you fall in love every time you see her at work in the flowerbeds.

Love blooms when we invest ourselves in one another's growth and development. For example, before I sat down to write this principle, I talked over the content with my husband. He nibbled on pistachios. I sipped some coffee. We both took notes and offered observations. We felt very close. To my way of thinking, it was a romantic moment because we were together in the same place—physically, emotionally and intellectually—in a way that was intimate, idiosyncratic and very "us."

If it sounds like *Real* love and romance grow in the midst of everyday living, that's because it does. Love doesn't depend on special occasions and grand gestures. It is there when you pick up the dry cleaning without being asked or buy that book because you know your partner or spouse will love it. It's in how you approach the little things as well as the big ones.

Although people like to believe you can be "lucky in love," luck is the least of it. Thomas Jefferson said, "I'm a great believer in luck, and I find the harder I work, the more I have of it." The same is true when it comes to loving relationships. The more time, effort, empathy and energy you put into them, the better they get.

This sentiment is echoed by poet Robert Browning who wrote, "Grow old along with me! The best is yet to be." If the best is "yet to be," then growing old together means always improving, evolving and deepening.

Although it is enduring and constant, there is nothing passive in *Real* love. It is active. It involves going out of your way to take care of someone you care about. If your partner is outside busting sod to create a new garden, get out there and grab a shovel. You'd be surprised how romantic a little sweat can be.

As a teenager, my friend Donna used to give copies of *The Velveteen Rabbit* to boys she wanted to date. When she told me about this, I asked her if she did it because she wanted to be loved as the Rabbit was loved. "Well, of course," she answered, "but I also wanted them to know that that's how I would love them."

As she grew older, Donna set aside Margery Williams's book and its message receded in her heart. When she began to think about finding a husband, she focused on external things such as looks, status and their potential for earning money. When she finally did marry, it was to a handsome fellow named Roger, who was studying to become a doctor.

At that time Donna was on her way to a career teaching at a college. The *Object* ideal of a college professor and a doctor who built a comfortable, high-status life together appealed to her very much and fit her preconceived notion of a perfect and successful relationship.

But college professors aren't paid very much and few get the security of tenure. Some physicians rise straight to the top. Many, like Roger, struggle to pay off their education loans and build a practice.

Besides their career disappointments, Roger and Donna also had to cope with some of the less-than-perfect personal qualities they each brought to the relationship. Eventually they found themselves in couples counseling, struggling to learn how to love each other after their mutual fantasy of a perfect existence had dissolved.

Hard work slowly made both Donna and Roger more *Real.* And once this happened, the anger and disappointment Donna had felt about the loss of her generically ideal marriage faded. In its place she felt a deeper, stronger attraction and attachment to Roger. Instead of being upset about the fact that Roger didn't fit her fantasy, she came to admire his kindness, sincerity and pluck. She could empathize with his efforts to improve himself and provide the security they both wanted.

Donna didn't realize it, but she had gone full circle, embracing, then losing, and finally rediscovering the truths in *The Velveteen Rabbit.*

No discussion of romantic love is complete without at least a brief word about sexuality. Sex is a significant part of adult relationships, and it can bring people both enormous pleasure and, unfortunately, significant turmoil and conflict.

In my private practice, people often begin to talk

about sex by asking, "What is good sex?" They ask because they are so worried about being "good" at it that they're not enjoying themselves at all. One young woman who enjoyed a relationship with a man she liked very much put it this way: "I keep thinking that he knows what I do. If there's no mystery, nothing new and exciting, why would he want to 'do it' with me again?"

Our culture has brainwashed us into believing that sex is only good if it's with someone new and involves startling techniques. But good sex is lovemaking performed with generosity and enthusiasm. It is not a competition or an opportunity to display prowess. It is a moment to connect with your partner with complete emotional and physical empathy. Who is more empathetic, a lover who has come to know his partner's body over time, or a sex partner on the first date?

Real love, which invites people to be themselves and show their passion without fear, is the answer to all the appearance and performance anxieties that plague sex in our time. And since it is based on empathy for people as individuals, *Real* love also has the potential to give you far more sexual happiness. Empathy allows us to sense another person's experience and *Real* lovers are so attuned to their partner's bodies and their responses that their technique gets better all the time. Would you rather be involved with someone who tunes into your individual desires and needs? Or do you want someone to treat you like just another generic man or woman?

While empathy improves intimacy, it is only part of the process. *Real* love encourages honesty and courage, which allows people to express their sexual needs and respond to them. It also builds both trust and self-esteem. When you feel good about yourself, and trust your sexual partner, you can relax and lose yourself in a way that's impossible when you are worried about your cellulite.

If it sounds to you like I'm suggesting that *Real* love among adult partners is better than the steamy stuff you see on the screen, then you understand me clearly. This is the kind of sex that ages well, keeps us close, and brings pleasure without angst and anxiety.

Velveteen

Principle #12

Real Is Ethical

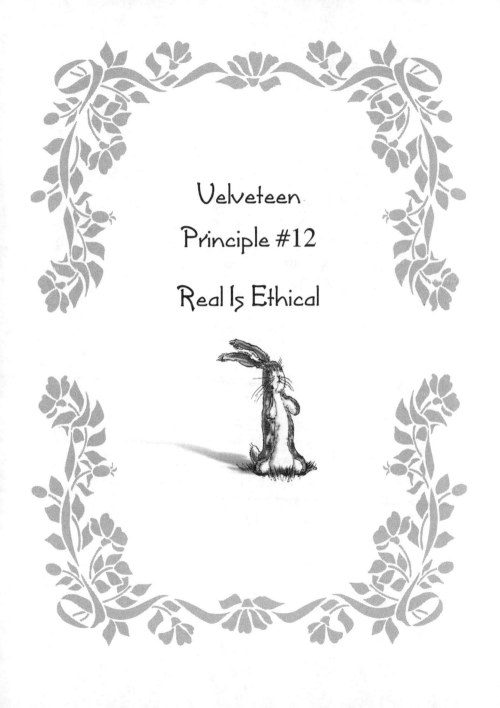

And so time went on, and the little Rabbit was very happy—so happy that he never noticed his beautiful velveteen fur was getting shabbier and shabbier, and his tail was coming unsewn. And all the pink rubbed off his nose where the Boy had kissed him.

The process of becoming *Real* eventually makes us calmly content with ourselves, which means we no longer feel overwhelmed by self-consciousness and self-doubt. We are so comfortable in our worth as human beings that we are able to act according to our highest values in a way that is practically automatic.

Almost without trying, we begin to act in ways that are consistently ethical. This happens because we are free of shame and no longer feel the need to misrepresent ourselves, act dishonestly or seek to make others feel insignificant. Ethical behavior, after all, involves being conscious of how our actions ripple out like little waves to affect others, and then acting to minimize the harm we do and maximize the good.

A mundane example of conscious decision-making arises when you reach for a stick of gum as you walk down the street. What do you do with the little foil wrapper? If you throw it on the ground, you begin a negative chain reaction. Taxpayers must put up cash to pay someone to clean up after you. Put it in your pocket, or throw it in a trash can, and you've made the ethical choice.

Of course, life presents us with far more challenging issues than what to do with a gum wrapper. I'm not able to tell you what to do with the touchiest problems, but I am suggesting that on a day-to-day basis, you can consciously choose the higher road.

A wonderfully succinct description of everyday ethics is expressed by the Golden Rule, which tells us to "Do unto others, as you would have them do unto you." The Golden Rule requires first for us to have self-empathy, in order to know how we hope to be treated. It then calls on us to transform that empathy into behavior that stresses human equality. This is the most basic form of ethics I can imagine.

The magic in this process—**self-empathy + empathy for others = ethical behavior**—is that it happens almost automatically. In fact, as soon as you start noticing that other people are not *Objects* but precious, worthy people, you'll try hard to avoid hurting them. You will be more courteous, more patient, more understanding and more encouraging of others. A student of mine explained how becoming *Real* made him a more ethical person during one of the most emotional classroom encounters I have ever had.

First, a little background: Jim had attended one of my group seminars the previous year. In that class, he had impressed everyone with stories of his travels around the world and acquisition of expensive toys. He worked for an airline, and his life seemed quite glamorous. Everything about him seemed to demonstrate that he was a shinier, brighter, more valuable *Object* than the other students in the class. As a consequence, he was impatient with others and did not show much respect for their efforts.

A year later, I looked at the roster for another study group and noticed that Jim would again be my student. I recalled his intelligence and energy, but also wondered if he would again be insensitive.

I was happy to discover that the Jim who appeared in this second study group was quieter and more attentive.

He was much more interested in others, and he even looked softer and more friendly. Students who had seen Jim before were as impressed as I was with the changes we observed. Eventually someone actually said something about his new attitude.

Jim explained that the change had been the result of a crisis. His daughter had been diagnosed with cancer. He quickly realized that none of the superficial things he once valued—appearance, money, possessions, fancy trips—could ease his daughter's suffering or his own anguish. All she wanted and needed was his attention and care. Driven by the love he felt for her, he stuck by her through every hospitalization, every treatment and her long recovery. He learned how to listen, how to share his heartfelt feelings and how to find the good in every moment. Watching his daughter struggle, and seeing other children do the same, changed his outlook on life.

"I can't believe that I used to think all the stuff I had and the things I did were so important," he confessed.

With some discomfort, he said that his daughter's terrible year had given him the gift of empathy, and it made it possible for him to treat everyone he encountered with more kindness. He had learned to be honest, courageous and compassionate.

"You know, it's strange," he said, "and a little embarrassing—but I'm a better person now than I was before." He didn't put it this way, but I would say that it happened because he had become *Real*.

When you have *Real* empathy and practice honesty, your emotions will often serve as a sensitive guide to the most ethical choice in a given situation. Many of the unsettling feelings we experience in our daily lives are actually signals that alert us to choices that violate our internal ethical standards. The little shudder of guilt you feel when a cashier gives you too much change, and you start to walk away, is coming from your *Real* self. If you experience anxiety as you mail off that not-so-honest tax return, that's your *Real* self, calling out to you. And do I have to describe how and why people feel shame when they betray a friend, spouse or colleague?

When we are engaged with other people on a direct and personal level, it is relatively easy to recognize moments when an ethical choice is at hand. Sometimes the mere act of noticing that another human being is involved gives us the emotional signals we need to be fair, open and honest. Look into the eyes of the person you are dealing with, and you'll see whether they feel they are being treated fairly.

More difficult are the choices with mixed consequences. Do you hire a contractor who uses laborers who do not have legal status? They need the money, and you could save on the cost of the job. The ethical choice here is not easy. It is up to you to decide if those pluses outweigh the negatives attached to participating in the underground economy. But if you are *Real*, you will at least reflect on the issues involved and own up to the decision rather than ignore its implications.

The same kind of conscious, thoughtful process can be used whenever we make choices that reach beyond the personal realm. Many organizations—workplaces, schools, religious congregations, service groups—can function within a framework of human empathy.

It is even possible to employ empathy and person-centered ethics in business. I know that businesses exist to make money and that when they do, employees and owners both benefit. But we all want to work in a place where we are respected, where we have opportunities to be creative and where we can take responsibility for our little corner of the company. A boss who is not afraid of being ethical will create this kind of work environment and will treat employees with unwavering fairness. The result is almost always a loyal workforce that performs more effectively, efficiently and profitably.

No discussion of *Real* ethics would be complete if we ignored the importance of maintaining our integrity and sticking up for what we value, even if it brings us into conflict with others. There is, in each of us, a set of values that we will not compromise. We betray what is *Real* if we fail to speak up in order to maintain a false sense of agreement.

I make this point whenever someone asks me for advice on a difficult problem. I say, "Do what will allow you to respect yourself tomorrow." This attitude contradicts the values of the *Object* culture, where lots of people believe: "It's not wrong unless you get caught." Deep inside, you can feel the difference between right and wrong, and you will always feel better when you are loyal to those feelings.

For example, when I am with someone who insults women, men, or a certain race or ethnic group, I speak up in a calm, gentle way. Usually I'll say something like, "You might want to check out your audience. Not everyone here has the same point of view," or "Please don't assume I agree with you on this." Fortunately, I find that this kind of honesty often brings an apology and, hopefully, a civilized discussion. When it doesn't, I don't engage in a big argument. That's not the point. I accept the moment of discomfort. And I am left feeling grateful both for my clearness of mind and the experience of learning about others. *Real* people don't expect agreement everywhere; *Real* embraces differences, even uncomfortable ones.

You have your own set of *Real* values that you will express when the moment requires. Maybe you think loyalty is a paramount value, or nonviolence, or love of country. If it is a deeply felt value, you won't be comfortable hiding it in the presence of others. You don't have to pick a fight or impose what you believe on others. But if you are *Real*, you won't want to betray yourself by hiding or pretending to agree when something important is at stake.

Although this last kind of ethical honesty may seem difficult right now, when you have done the work to identify your *Real* self, you gain confidence and courage. You also acquire a broader, more understanding view of all aspects of human nature. This knowledge will allow you to be calmly honest without being argumentative, confrontational or hurtful. In the end, this honesty will make others feel more relaxed in your presence because they know the *Real* you.

Epilogue

Real Has Meaning

That night he was almost too happy to sleep, and so much love stirred in his little sawdust heart that it almost burst. And into his boot-button eyes that had long ago lost their polish, there came a look of wisdom and beauty, so that even Nana noticed it next morning when she picked him up and said, "I declare if that old Bunny hasn't got quite a knowing expression!"

After he became *Real*, the Velveteen Rabbit looked upon the world with the quiet wisdom we acquire when we have grown enough and learned enough to understand what *Really* fulfills and sustains us as unique individuals. To put it another way, we know what gives our lives true value and meaning. This is the ultimate goal we reach as we mature as *Real* people.

The hunger for a sense of meaning—for true value—is universal and as old as humanity itself. We all want to feel that we have a purpose and that our presence on this planet matters. In the U.S. of G. this desire is dismissed as impractical and even frivolous. But when you are *Real*, the quest for meaning is central to your life. It leads you to nurture your own values, interests and passions and to connect with others in empathetic and positive relationships.

This doesn't happen without some effort. A *Real* life demands your active participation. It docsn't happen *to* you. You design it and then create it. *Real* doesn't mean you'll be perfect at anything. It means that you're willing to grow and learn through experience. And as a result, you know that you always did your best.

Besides saving us from regrets, a life conducted in this *Real* way creates a beautiful and unique story that becomes our legacy to the people we love and, perhaps, to people we never knew. This is the greatest reward of living as a *Real* person. It's not stuff or power or achievement, but rather a sense that you are using your time on Earth well, that you are connected to others and that your life matters.

Once you are *Real*, and you know that everything you say and do matters, you can also understand that we each leave a mark on the world that remains long after we're gone. Whether we recognize it or not, we all create a legacy.

A *Real* legacy is not something tangible—cash, stocks and bonds, real estate, art—or even a reputation that translates into status for our loved ones. Instead, a *Real* legacy is the example you set in life, which will be evident in the stories people tell about you long after you are gone.

To get some idea of the legacy you are creating, listen carefully to what people say about you now—the little stories they tell—and also how they tell them. If I use myself as an example, I can report that my friends and family tend to tease me lovingly about my foibles—my terrible sense of direction, my FEMA tendencies—but they also talk about my effort to nurture what is *Real*, to be honest, empathetic and brave, despite my doubts and fears.

Every life is, ultimately, a story with a message. This is true, even when it comes to fictional characters whose lives are drawn in books by gifted authors. In writing *The Velveteen Rabbit,* Margery Williams sketched for us a childlike character who expresses the hopes, dreams, anxieties and fears we have all experienced at one time or another. Then she lets the Velveteen Rabbit explore life and strive to become *Real* in a way that captures our hearts and inspires us to do the same. The Rabbit is brave, honest and empathetic, and we identify with him in many ways. He is also part of Margery Williams's own legacy, a magnificent gift enjoyed by millions of people that makes me grateful that she walked this Earth as a *Real* person.

If you become more *Real* in your own life and bring that to your relationships, you are practically guaranteed to leave behind an inspiring example for others. Your life's message will encourage everyone you touch to live with a sense of wonder, curiosity and openness, rather than cynicism and fear. It will say, "I was *Real*. And you can be *Real,* too."

What meaning will you discover as you create a legacy? Be *Real* in your own, unique way, and you will find out.

"I suppose you are Real?" said the Rabbit. And then he wished he had not said it, for he thought the Skin Horse might be sensitive. But the Skin Horse only smiled. "The Boy's uncle made me Real," he said. "That was a great many years ago; but once you are Real, you can't become unreal again. It lasts for always."

We're all ears . . .

. . . and we love to hear Real comments
and Real stories from Real readers.
To become part of our community of Real,
please visit:

www.velveteenprinciples.com